Black, John
The Art of history

DATE DUE

FEB 18 '91			
APR 2 2 '97			
NOV 2 4 '97			
JUN 2 5 1998			

THE ART OF HISTORY

THE
ART OF HISTORY

A STUDY OF
FOUR GREAT HISTORIANS OF
THE EIGHTEENTH CENTURY

BY

J. B. BLACK, M.A.

NEW YORK
RUSSELL & RUSSELL · INC
1965

FIRST PUBLISHED IN 1926
REISSUED, 1965, BY RUSSELL & RUSSELL, INC.
BY ARRANGEMENT WITH METHUEN & CO., LTD., LONDON
L.C. CATALOG CARD NO: 65—18790
PRINTED IN THE UNITED STATES OF AMERICA

CONTENTS

To
MY PUPILS PAST AND PRESENT

PREFACE

THIS book does not profess to be a discussion of eighteenth century historiography in general; its object is specific, viz., to examine sympathetically and critically, the ideas entertained by Voltaire, Hume, Robertson, and Gibbon, with respect to the theory and practice of the historical art. At the same time, an attempt has been made in the *Introduction* to throw into relief the chief differences between the ideals of this literary-philosophical school and those which prevail among historians to-day; and perhaps a word is necessary concerning the standpoint from which the argument has been conducted. The assumption on which it rests, and indeed the motive lying behind the entire essay, is that the intimate union between literature, philosophy, and history, so amply demonstrated in the writings of Voltaire and his "school," is not merely an ideal of the eighteenth century but one which bears a validity for all time. Or, more explicitly, history devoid of philosophic and literary interest, which concerns itself only with the establishment of the fact, however scientifically handled, has always seemed to the writer to be blind of an eye and lame of gait : a study, in short, of contracting horizons and diminishing cultural value. In the eighteenth century, history was written, not by "scientists" but by humanists, who brought to it the fruits of a ripe wisdom; and it would not be an exaggeration to say that under their aegis it became a complete and satisfying culture in itself. Is it permissible to believe that when the humanist has come into his own once more we shall see the subject, freed from excessive subserviency to "science," rise again to the commanding position it held in the days of Voltaire and Gibbon—the indispensable passport of every educated person, and a social force of the first magnitude ? Such, at any rate, is the belief underlying the following studies.

It is a pleasure to acknowledge our particular indebtedness in regard to the first two chapters: first, to Fueter's *Geschichte der neueren Historiographie*, the best general account of European historiography from the Renaissance onwards; secondly, to R. Mayr's *Voltaire Studien* (Wien, 1879); to S. Daiches' *Uber das Verhaltnis der Geschichtsschreibung*; *D. Hume's zu seiner praktischen Philosophie* (Leipzig, 1903); to J. Goldstein's *Die empiristische Geschichtsauffassung David Hume's* (Leipzig, 1903); and to H. Goebel's *Das Philosophische in Hume's Geschichte von England* (Marburg, 1897). It may be added, however, that although these writers have covered the ground attempted in the chapters on Voltaire and Hume, they have not taken the place of independent investigation, nor precluded a fresh handling of the subject. In each case the writings of the authors themselves have formed the basis of the discussion.

The references in the text are to the following works:

Voltaire, *Œuvres*, Paris, 1877–85 (52 vols.).
Hume, *History of England*, London, 1782 (8 vols.).
　　　Philosophical Works, Edinburgh, 1826 (4 vols.).
　　　A Treatise of Human Nature, ed. Selby-Bigge, 1896.
　　　Enquiries, ed. Selby-Bigge, 1902.
Robertson, *Works*, ed. Lynam, 1826 (6 vols.).
Gibbon, *The Decline and Fall of the Roman Empire*, ed.
　　　J. B. Bury, 1900 (7 vols.).
　　　Miscellaneous Works, ed. Lord Sheffield, 1815
　　　(3 vols.).
　　　Autobiography, ed. G. Birkbeck Hill, 1897.

J. B. BLACK

Sheffield, January 1926

THE ART OF HISTORY

INTRODUCTION

§ I

HISTORIOGRAPHY, or the art of writing history, is a term to which it is impossible to assign a content that will apply equally to all periods. Like most conceptions outside the narrow range of mathematical science, it depends, to a large degree, on the general intellectual environment to which it stands related, and of which it is, in some sense, a specialized product. It moves, so to speak, with that environment, and must be studied in conjunction with it; or, as Buckle once remarked,[1] "There will always be a connection between the way in which men contemplate the past and the way in which they contemplate the present." Here, at least, there is some approximation between the otherwise very different historical standpoints of the eighteenth and nineteenth centuries : both were profoundly affected by contemporary thought—the eighteenth by the philosophical movement known as the *Enlightenment*, the nineteenth by the vast progress of science and the doctrine of evolution. Thus, when Voltaire circulated his celebrated aphorism, *"Il faut écrire l'histoire en philosophe,"*[2] he gave currency to a view just as significant for the age in which he lived, as Ranke's more famous " *Er will bloss sagen wie es eigentlich gewesen* "[3] was for the succeeding century. Viewed in this light, as an off-shoot of the general intellectual development of an epoch, and bearing an organic relation

[1] *History of Civilisation in England*, I, p. 289.
[2] Voltaire à Thieriot, 31 Oct., 1738 ; cf. also *Œuvres* xxv, p. 169—" Jamais le public n'a mieux senti qu'il n'appartient qu'aux philosophes d'écrire l'histoire."
[3] *Geschichte der romanischen und germanischen Volker*, Vorrede.

to the whole, the eighteenth century attitude to history and the historical art is a topic of great interest.

But the interest is not merely historiographical. If the eighteenth century had a point of view in regard to the past, which is intimately bound up with the culture of the time, it is greatly to be doubted whether we do well, in our impetuous search for first-hand material, to dismiss the writers of the so-called Age of Reason—as we too frequently do—as if we had for ever transcended them. "The Man of taste," says Sainte-Beuve,[1] speaking of tradition in literature, "ought for his own sake, it seems to me, to return every four or five years upon the best of his old admirations, to verify them, to put them to the test again as though they were new." Is it not possible that, just as we "return upon" the general literature of the eighteenth century for the vigorous sense it displays, and the enrichment it brings to our common stock of literary canons, so, too, we may expect that historians of the calibre of Voltaire, Hume, and Gibbon have something to communicate to us concerning history, of more than merely contemporary and ephemeral interest? Every age, it may be assumed, whatever the state of its technical equipment, and whatever its errors as to fact may be, by interpreting the record of the past in the light of its own ideas, and in ways acceptable to itself, casts an illuminating beam athwart the course of history, which subsequent ages cannot repeat, and can only recapture with difficulty. In other words, there is an element in all great historical generalizations, which time does not stale nor criticism wholly subvert. The eighteenth century historians may have been amateurish and casual in their treatment of documents, sometimes childishly ignorant of the technique of research, and often perverse in their conclusions ; in fact, they may represent a descent in scholarship from the level attained in the preceding century ;[2] but the important thing about them is the fact that they applied the whole culture of the age in which they lived to what they *did know* of the past ; and this gives their books a substantiality and a depth of insight not uncommonly

[1] *Causeries du Lundi*, Vol. XV, p. 379.
[2] Fueter : *Geschichte der neueren Historiographie*, pp. 245-6.

lacking even in the "scientific" histories of more recent times. At any rate, the clues they continually throw out as to the meaning of events are not without their value to modern historians. Probably some such thought as this passed through the mind of Professor Whitney when he penned the following defence of "secondary writers." "History," he remarks,[1] "is its own interpreter. Each successive generation sees some aspect of the original evidence which it alone can understand. . . . We cannot afford to neglect our predecessors. Very often from a secondary writer we get a clue or a suggestion, which, as we think it over along with our original authorities, illuminates a tangled period, or a darkened corner."

Perhaps the most arresting characteristic of Voltaire and his "school" is the belief they had in the ethical nature of their task. They conceived that they held a trust for humanity, not only to delineate faithfully what happened in the past, but also to weigh it in the balances of the present, to assess its value, and to discriminate between what is culturally worth remembering and what is not. In pursuance of this conviction they boldly applied their standards and criteria to all ages, peoples, and events, and produced a history that appealed to their readers, because it was, in reality, as much a part of the living present as a novel or a drama. To-day the frontiers of his subject have been drawn more closely about the historian ; his function, it is said, is to concern himself with the past as a purely objective phenomenon, to describe what took place, *in situ* as it were, or (as some would prefer to put it) in its evolutionary setting, much as a scientist might describe the history of the solar system, or the evolution of the planet, and to leave the ultimate assessment—if such an assessment be possible and desirable —to the philosopher and the religious dogmatist.[2] The

[1] *An Inaugural Address*, by Prof. J. P. Whitney, Cambridge, 1919.
[2] Bernheim : *Lehrbuch der historischen Methode*, p. 151—" Die Geschichtswissenschaft hat es nur mit der kausalen Erforschung und Darlegung der Entwicklung zu tun, nicht mit deren letzten Grunden."
Langlois and Seignobos : *Introduction to the Study of History*—" The naturalist might express his sympathy with or his admiration for an animal. . . . But it is obvious that in history, as in every other subject, judgments of this kind are foreign to science " (note, p. 279).
Cf. also F. York Powell, *Preface* to Langlois and Seignobos.

prohibition, of course, is not absolute ; for even the most resolute upholder of scientific history would not deny the legitimacy of passing judgments on characters and events, provided these judgments are based upon standards which the actors had consciously or subconsciously before them : that is, provided they have a sound documentary foundation. It is only with judgments imported from the outside, and based upon an ethic the actors would not have acknowledged, that the historian, in the opinion of the modern realist school, ought not to concern himself ; he has no right, they say, to summon the past before the bar of the present—his duty is to explain it, and there his work ends. " Like the physical sciences and all other branches of knowledge," writes Professor Bury,[1] " history requires for its scientific development complete freedom and independence ; its value is annulled and its powers are paralysed if it consents to be ancillary to politics, ethics, or theology ; in order to fulfil its function, it must (like all sciences) be treated as if it were an end in itself."

Now, obviously, this is one of the consequences of specialization, and the differentiation of functions in the field of science and letters. Only by carefully delimiting the frontiers of subjects is it possible for investigators to grasp what their task is, and to work at it with confidence and tenacity : a blurred vision means defective workmanship. It must also be admitted that the gains made under the new dispensation have been enormous : in accuracy, fullness, and depth, our knowledge of the past far outranges the limited vision of the eighteenth century. But the penalties paid for this wonderful advance must not be ignored. We have discovered, in the process of investigation, that the facts of history are infinite in number ; and if, as a French historian assures us,[2] they are " everything," the labour of collecting and interpreting them becomes infinite also. In fact, there is presented to us the impressive spectacle of whole armies of collaborators grappling with the great historical synthesis of the future, and the individual sinking into comparative insignificance.

---

[1] *The Ancient Greek Historians*, p. 245.
[2] M. Giry : Preface to Lot, *Les Derniers Carolingiens*—" Dans l'histoire le détail c'est tout."

And a question naturally suggests itself. Assuming that the final synthesis will be achieved—at present it is a matter of faith—may we presume that it will be, not only comprehensive, but readable and compassable as well? If so, who will read, comprehend, and compass it? In the eighteenth century the study of history was well within the scope of every educated person; to-day it is written by specialists primarily for specialists, and little attempt is made to canvass intellectual interests outside the circle of the initiated: indeed, efforts of this nature might be, and are, frowned upon as a dereliction of duty. In the future, if we may judge by the collaborative works at present in circulation, it is probable that the task of assimilation will be more difficult than ever; and history may lose any value it possesses as an element in the cultural life of the community. Surely this is a contingency rather to be deplored. The late Lord Morley probably exaggerated when he penned the following indictment; but his words are worth recalling for the strong seasoning of truth they contain. "It may perhaps be contended," he writes,[1] "that the conception of history has, on the whole, gone back rather than advanced within the last hundred years. There have been signs in our own day of its becoming narrow, pedantic, and trivial. It threatens to degenerate from a broad survey of great periods and movements of human societies into vast and countless accumulations of insignificant facts, sterile knowledge, and frivolous antiquarianism, in which the spirit of epochs is lost, and the direction, meaning, and summary of the various courses of human history all disappear."

But there is another penalty attaching to this narrowing of the historian's field of vision, hardly less to be deplored. We have partially lost sight of the relation of history to other universes of thought, and in particular to the ethical universe.

---

[1] Morley: *Diderot*, pp. 378-9; cf. also Leslie Stephen: *Studies of a Biographer*, I (" National Biography ")—" It may be doubted whether this huge accumulation of materials has been an unmixed blessing to history. . . . We feel sometimes that it is possible to have too much State-paper. The main outlines, which used to be the whole of history, are still the most important, and instead of being filled up and rendered more precise and vivid, they sometimes seem to disappear behind an elaborate account of what statesmen and diplomatists happened to think about them at the time," etc.

On every side one hears the academic historian deny that his subject matter has anything to do with philosophy. Yet it seems scarcely conceivable that the last word on any event, movement, or character, in history can be merely a record *de ce qui était*; such a record, out of touch with contemporary life, must always be barren, dead, and valueless. Perhaps we might hazard the opinion that " History for history's sake," like the corresponding formula " Art for Art's sake," is one of those hot-house growths which flourish only in the unreal atmosphere of institutions that are themselves out of touch with realities. At any rate, if the valuation of the past is not attempted by the historian, it will be effected by someone whose acquaintance with the subject-matter of history is, in all likelihood, scanty and furtive.

The point is not entirely a theoretical one : teachers of history are perpetually confronted with the difficulty of assessing the events they discuss, according to some standards or principles which they must render more or less explicit. Again and again they find their subject running into ethics on the one hand, and political philosophy on the other. The inquiring pupil demands to know why Cæsar, Charlemagne, Cromwell, Frederick the Great, Napolean, Cecil Rhodes, or any one of a hundred other " heroes " is to be placed in the Pantheon of history as " one whom humanity must honour " ; and he will not be fobbed off with references to " the necessities of the times," " national or imperial interests," " inherent supremacy of the white race," " indefeasibility of State sovereignity " or any other similar criterion of more or less limited validity. On the contrary, he wants to *passer outre*, to relate the transactions he has studied to some " good " which stands outside them, challenges comparison with them, and is related, at the same time, to his own ethical belief. If this is not accomplished for him by the teacher, or at least indicated, he is left at the mercy of his own *implicit* assumptions, which he has never tested, and possibly never made the subject of an inquiry at all. And history becomes a kind of puzzle capable of being correctly articulated, but lacking meaning as a whole, because it has no background.

Now the eighteenth century historians, whatever their other shortcomings may be, undoubtedly accomplished their assessment of the past with commendable vigour. There is never any doubt left in the mind of the reader what Voltaire or Hume, for example, think of the matters they describe. The important events of history are set in a wide framework, their bearings are indicated to the great moral background against which the drama of the race is enacted, and they are judged with respect to standards which the writers, rightly or wrongly, regarded as ultimate. Hence it comes about that to all who look to history for more than factual instruction, who believe that a historical fact is not fully appreciated until it is placed in its philosophical as well as its purely causal relationships, the historians of the Age of Reason will never quite lose their charm ; on the contrary, they will remain as perhaps the most brilliant examples of how humane culture may be brought into fruitful contact with what would otherwise be a dead and, for the vast majority, a valueless past.

So far, it will be observed, we have said nothing about the contention that history is a science. The reason is not very far to seek. Taken in its widest sense, that is, as covering *all* the operations of the historian, this assumption becomes less and less tenable, as the concepts and methods which the historian employs as aids in his analysis and synthesis are submitted to examination. The stanchest defender of the " science of history " would not now contend that there is any real comparison between his subject and the sciences proper. How could there be, when the historian is in the position of a scientist who receives information about the results of his experiments " from his laboratory boy ? " " An historical statement," says M. Seignobos [1] " is, in the most favourable case, but an indifferently made observation " ; and again, [2] " From the very nature of its materials history is necessarily a *subjective* science ; " and still more significantly, [3] " *Every historical image contains a large part of fancy.*" But it would be wearisome to reopen the old con-

---

[1] *Introduction to the Study of History*, p. 196.
[2] *Ibid.*, p. 217.
[3] *Ibid.*, p. 222.

troversy. That there is no such thing as an "established" science of history must be apparent from the fact that history has not yet invented a nomenclature or a standardized vocabulary : it possesses only a jargon, which varies from writer to writer, in much the same way as the ordinary language of literature. Moreover, in spite of its claims to the contrary, it is full of implicit assumptions, is still written from "standpoints," and, in short, is never entirely free from distortion by personal bias. Few, at any rate, would now agree with Ranke and Lord Acton that it is possible to write a completely objective account of any historical transaction, however remote. The great work the latter planned is ample proof that the belief, noble as it was, bore little correspondence with the actual circumstances under which history must, perforce, be written. At best, then, the doctrine that history is a science must be regarded as merely a regulative rule, a working hypothesis, a by-law, and not an absolute and inflexible principle : an ideal rather than a description of fact, and like all ideals—only approximately attainable.[1]

Perhaps we might go further and assert that the "subjectivity" of history is, in the nature of things, not only ineradicable, but also, if properly controlled, advantageous. When the constructive work of the historian—as distinct from the documentary—is analysed in detail, it will generally be found that his understanding of the past is largely dependant upon his understanding of the present.[2] As we deepen our knowledge of the social, political, and economic phenomena with which we are surrounded, as we multiply our categories of classification, and explore the inter-relation of the forces and factors, both psychic and material, which go to the production of individual acts, or events, or movements, so, too, we increase the number of clues at our disposal for penetrating the secret of the past. In fact, there is no other procedure open to us. Direct observation of historical events is out of the question : they must always be seen indirectly, reflected, so to speak, in the mirror of the present ; and the

[1] Berheim : *Lehrbuch*, pp. 762-76, where the following significant admission is made : "Auch der Historiker kann und soll sich eines bestimmten Standpunktes nicht Entschlagen " (p. 763).
[2] Langlois and Seignobos, pp. 222 9.

historian is compelled to form his picture of what happened
in past times, on the analogy of modern events with which
he is immediately acquainted. In other words, he must
have a " philosophy of history," a reasoned conception of
how things actually happen, before he is in a position to
interpret any historical event. It would also appear to
follow that his depth of insight into the past is conditioned
by the depth of his knowledge of the world in which he lives.
" The point of view of the historian," says Professor Bury,[1]
" is conditioned by the mentality of his own age ; the focus
of his vision is determined within narrow limits by the conditions of contemporary civilisation. There can be nothing
final about his judgments, and their permanent interest lies
in the fact that they are judgments pronounced at a given
epoch and are characteristic of the tendencies and ideas of
that epoch." If so, what becomes of his pure objective
contemplation ?

To the student of historiography nothing is more instructive
than to observe the degree to which history in the nineteenth
century has been affected by subjective and pragmatic considerations. It is not an exaggeration to say that in the vast
majority of cases, if not actually in all, the objective and
contemplative ideal has been heavily overborne by subjectivism and utilitarianism of one sort or another. In fact,
the greatest writers of the century—those who have made
their mark not only as stylists but also as contributors to
the advance of historical knowledge—have been the most
deeply concerned with the " philosophy " of events. Thus,
Hallam and Macaulay were Whigs ; and their works, however
much they differ in the degree to which they show it, bear on
their face the unmistakable sign manual of Whig political
philosophy.[2] To Seeley, history was avowedly a school of
politics, in which every budding statesman ought to graduate.
" In dealing with history," writes Prothero,[3] " he always
kept a definite end in view—the solution of some problem,
the establishment of some principle, which would arrest the

[1] *The Ancient Greek Historians*, p. 252.
[2] Gooch : *History and Historians in the Nineteenth Century*, pp. 283 and 302.
[3] *Ibid.*, p. 373.

attention of the student, and might be of use to the statesman." Lecky's political views, again, shine through the
pages of his Irish history, albeit he did more than most to
preserve the impartiality of the judge.[1] Freeman wrote under
the influence of his favourite doctrine that the essence of
history is continuity, and the essence of continuity, politics ;
and deliberately ignored the social, economic, and ideological
aspects of the subjects he treated.[2] Than Lord Acton there
was probably never a historian who grasped more firmly, or
more trenchantly expressed, the conviction that history is a
great moral teacher. " The great achievement of history,"
he wrote, " is to develop, perfect, and arm conscience." " I
exhort you," he remarks in his *Study of History*, " never to
debase the moral currency, but to try others by the same
maxim that governs your own lives, and to suffer no man and
no cause to escape the undying penalty which history has the
power to inflict on wrong." Sismondi was equally emphatic
on the moral mission of the historian. " There is for the
historian," he writes,[3] " a holier mission than of working to
extend the renown of a great people, and that is to judge
every event by the great touchstone of the laws of morality."

Of the great Germans who followed Ranke—Mommsen,
Sybel, Treitschke—it is now a commonplace to say that they
were all immersed in the seething cauldron of German politics,
and consciously subordinated their teaching as historians to
the needs of the Fatherland. To Mommsen, the end of the
historic process is *Kultur* ; and if, in the struggle to establish
it, weak nations go to the wall, it is only in obedience to
Nature's law : history is the supreme tribunal of the world,
and the sole criterion of a nation's value is success. Thus,
the History of Rome is essentially a pæan to the memory of
Cæsar,[4] a glorification of *Macht* as the maker of States.
Sybel's more fiery temper was compounded of three ingredients
—antipathy to France, hatred of Jesuits, and love of Prussia ;
and his most impressive work, the *History of the French
Revolution*, is a sustained attempt, under the guise of scientific

[1] Gooch : *History and Historians in the Ninteenth Century*, p. 367.
[2] Bryce : *Studies in Contemporary Biography*, p. 268.
[3] Gooch, p. 167.
[4] Guilland : *Modern Germany and her Historians*, p. 158

impartiality, to decry the greatest event in modern history, to destroy its glamour, and to arrest the progress of Liberalism in Germany.[1] Treitschke, again, was a pronounced publicist, and he made no effort to hide the subjective and pragmatic character of his *History of Germany in the Nineteenth Century.* "Only a stout heart," he wrote,[2] "which feels the joys and sorrows of the Fatherland as its own, can give veracity to an historical narrative"; and again, "The impressive power of a historical work always lies in the vigorous personality of the historian."

Much the same holds good of the leading lights in Italian history during the century. One and all they wrote their works under the flaming impulse of the struggle with Austria, or with this as a background to their thinking, their object being to stimulate the youths of the nation to a proper appreciation of their glorious heritage. Of Amari's *History of the Sicilian Vespers* Dr. Gooch writes [3] " While recording the expulsion of the French, he and his readers were thinking of the Neapolitan Bourbons." Balbo's *Summary of Italian History,* according to the same writer,[4] was " beyond everything else a contribution to the education of the national consciousness."

Finally, let us take the two historians who approached, in the opinion of most critics, most nearly to the ideal of pure objectivity, viz. Ranke and Stubbs. There is not the slightest doubt that both made unremitting efforts to keep their personal views separate from their professional opinions, and to a remarkable degree they succeeded. Yet, subsequent criticism has shown that the alleged objectivity was a hallucination : each had his standpoint and his controlling ideas of which he could not divest himself any more than he could escape from his skin. Ranke's conception of history reposed on the assumption that the evolution of States is the capital fact in modern history—that State and nation are one and the same thing. Hence his studies were directed primarily to the elucidation of the ways in which States are built up,

---

[1] *Ibid.,* p. 184.
[2] Treitschke : *Deutsche Geschichte im 19 Jahrhundert,* 1913, Vol. IV, p. 471.
[3] *History and Historians,* p. 437.
[4] *Ibid.,* p. 438.

and he selected those periods in the history of the nations when the formative forces were at their greatest strength. " The historian, in his judgment," writes Professor Guilland,[1] " had no other mission than to fortify political judgment." Stubbs has also fallen from his pedestal of neutrality. It appears, that he too, was subjective and pragmatical. He had formed his mind, says Petit-Dutaillis,[2] on the prevalent Germanism and liberalism of the age in which he wrote. Taking his cue from German historians who traced all political liberty to the primitive institutions of their race, " he thought he saw in the development of the English Constitution the magnificent and unique expansion of these first germs of self-government, and England was for him the ' messenger of liberty to the world.' " The bias due to these prepossessions is unmistakably visible in his handling of Magna Charta and the earlier development of the Constitution ; on both points he has long been superseded.

It is unnecessary to draw the moral. Pragmatism and subjectivism seem to be ineradicably embedded in the matter of history ; and instead of rebelling against them as evils, it might be wiser for us to accept them as part and parcel of our stock-in-trade. Two conclusions, however, may be drawn from what has been said. In the first place, if history is its own interpreter, if the drama of the past can only be seen through the spectacles provided by the present, it cannot be known *absolutely* : it can only be known *relatively*. It is not, as Dr. Barker recently affirmed,[3] a " fixed *datum*," but " a Protean thing, which can change from shape to shape according to the phase of the spirit in which it is present." Moreover, this would be so even if all the documents were published, and the *data* exposed before us like an open book ; there would still be the incalculable factor of the present to contend with ; and our picture of what happened in the past would continue to be modified in the light of new ideas thrown up from time to time by the examination of contemporary phenomena. If there is a particle of truth in the

[1] *Modern Germany and her Historians*, p. 96.
[2] *Studies Supplementary to Stubbs*, Preface, p. xiii.
[3] *Address to the Historical Association*, reprinted in " History," July, 1922.

Crocean conception that the only history worth considering is history written frankly from the standpoint of the present [1] —" contemporary history "—there is some justification for adopting a less severe attitude to the so-called foibles of Voltaire and his followers. The standpoint of the eighteenth century was simply an exaggeration of that which every historian must adopt if he hopes to write a complete account of any historical event. It attempted to penetrate the labyrinth of the past by exploring it in the light of ideas current in Europe at the time ; and despite all its sins of omission it accomplished its task with great brilliancy and not a little success.

In the second place, the belief held by the historians of the eightheenth century that it was only those who had mingled in affairs who could legitimately hope to write history as it should be written, when viewed in conjunction with the foregoing remarks, does not appear to be a fallacy, but a useful corrective to overmuch abstraction and an additional source of illumination. Knowledge of human nature, familiarity at first hand with the actual working of institutions, the power " to mount up from men's actions to their motives, and to descend again from their motives to their actions " [2]—all this is grist to the mill of the historian ; and it is not the sort of grist that comes from documents. The greatness of the eighteenth century lies in the fact that it was prepared to fuse history with other universes of knowledge, to seek and apply the clues which science, and philosophy, and practical experience, were in a position to place in its hands, and at the same time not to abate one jot or tittle of the care which the study demanded of its devotees.

It will not be concluded that what we advocate is a return to the practices and methods of the eighteenth century : far from it. The vast apparatus of research, the steady multiplication of reliable documents, the continuous sub-division of labour—all this is irrefragibly established ; and

[1] Croce : On History, p. 12 (English translation).
[2] Hume : Enquiry Concerning the Human Understanding, pp. 84-5 (Selby-Bigge, 1902).

no one in his sane senses would for a moment think of asking that it should be altered, any more than he would advocate a return to the age of the handmill or the hour-glass. It is not with this aspect of the subject that we are here concerned : the interest, for the moment, centres in the constructive part of the historians' work, which presupposes, and is only possible when, the documentary part has been accomplished. In this connexion, all that is suggested is that the pragmatic note might, with advantage, be more explicit than it is in the histories that are being written to-day. There is, in short, a need for the reintegration of history and philosophy, and the reintegration ought, this time, to come from the historian's side rather than the philosopher's. The important result of such a conjunction would be a great increase in the cultural value of the subject. In any case, the field of history is wide enough to admit of the attempt being made.

§ 2

IN all probability there has never been a period when history was so much in demand among the reading public in all European countries as the latter part of the eighteenth century.[1] It would be no exaggeration to say that the vogue of historical books between 1750 and the outbreak of the French Revolution was as great as the vogue of poetical literature in the age of Shakespeare or of the novel in the age of Scott. Every one read it and talked about it. When Voltaire's first work, *Charles XII*, appeared it was devoured with as much avidity as if it had been a romance, rather than a sober statement of fact ;[2] and the numerous piratical editions of his later histories suggest that the popularity of the writer in no way diminished as he grew older. Gibbon's success, again, was hardly less pronounced : the

---

[1] " L'histoire est la partie des belles-lettres qui a le plus de partisans dans tous les pays."—Voltaire à Cideville, 9 Juli, 1754.
" History is the most popular species of writing."—Gibbon : *Autobiography*, p. 194.
" I believe this to be the historical age and this the historical nation."—Hume : *Letters to Strahan*, p. 155.
[2] Lanson : *Voltaire*, p. 111.

Decline and Fall sold like a threepenny pamphlet on the affairs of the day. " My book," writes the proud author,[1] "was on every table, and on almost every toilet : the historian was crowned by the taste and fashion of the day." " Upon my soul," exclaimed Garrick,[2] speaking of Robertson's *Scotland*, " I was never more entertained in my life. . . . I finished the three first books at two sittings." A more distinguished compliment was paid to the same writer's *Charles V* by the Empress Catherine of Russia, who apparently carried it about with her on her long journeys through the empire. " I never leave off reading it," she wrote,[3] " especially the first volume." As for Hume, his fame was slower in being established in England, because of his anti-Whig bias and his laudation of Charles I ; but in Paris he reaped a whirlwind of applause, and became the lion of the hour in every *salon* of note. " They will drive me out of France," he commented,[4] " *à coup de complimens et de louanges.*"

The explanation of this remarkable popularity of history lies, happily, on the surface. To begin with, we must bear in mind that, in the eighteenth century, it was quite natural and proper to speak of history as literature, or, at all events, a branch of literature. The globe of human knowledge was still intact and fairly safe from the ravages of specialism ; and writers moved about freely among the arts and sciences, with an easy gaiety and a sureness of step, that seem, by contrast with the laboured progression of to-day, little short of marvellous. At the present time specialism begins in the school, and the instruction of the future historian in the use of his tools is entered upon during his university career. He is introduced as early as is feasible to diplomatic and palæography, acquainted with the manner in which documents should be handled, and launched on his voyage of discovery armed cap-à-pie with all the devices science has evolved. In the eighteenth century, on the other hand, vocational training of this nature was practically non-existent, and the budding historian had to make shift to pick up his equipment

[1] *Autobiog.*, p. 195.
[2] Stewart : *Life of Robertson*, pp. 114-15.
[3] *Ibid.*, p. 231, note.
[4] Burton : *Life and Letters of David Hume*, II, p. 172. *Ibid.*, pp. 176-7.

as he went along. It must remain an interesting historical fact that the great Gibbon knew next to nothing of the so-called auxiliary sciences on which history depends; or he knew enough only to pass off his ignorance with a joke. "Nor should I complain," he noted in his *Autobiography*,[1] "of the intricacy of Greek abbreviations and Gothic alphabets, since every day, in a familiar language, I am at a loss to decipher the hieroglyphics of a female note." The consequence was that in the absence of specialist training the basis of historical research was simply a wide and generous culture, and every man of letters who felt he possessed this deemed himself capable of trying his hand at what was then described as "historical composition." Nor was it an accident that the leading historians of the eighteenth century were all men who wandered into history in their maturity. Whatever else may be said about them, this at least is true, that their books represent the culmination of their entire mental development, rather than the researches of the few years that often went to their production. What they brought to history from the storehouse of general knowledge is just as important as what they evolved from it; in other words, the interpretation they were able to put upon the facts, fallacious as it frequently was, provides the central core of interest in their books. Thus, for example, Voltaire was a scientist, a philosopher, a poet, and a dramatist before he turned to the study of historical documents and became the historiographer of France. Hume could lay claim to being an economist [2] and a philosopher of note, as well as a brilliant essayist, before he plunged into the recesses of the Advocates' Library and produced his *History of England*. And Gibbon, albeit more of a specialist than either Voltaire or Hume, approached his life-task only after repeated efforts to establish his fame as a literary critic. As is well known, he was by choice and training a classical scholar rather than a historian, when the theme of his great work dawned upon him. One and all, the outstanding figures in the realm of

[1] Page 158.
[2] For the importance of Hume's economic studies, *vide* Bonar: *Philosophy and Political Economy*, pp. 105-29; and Burton: *Life and Correspondence of D. Hume*, I, pp. 357-63.

history, during this period, were primarily men of letters, and they grounded their appeal to the reading public more upon the broad sweep of their humanistic culture than upon their mastery of the technical apparatus of the professed historian. On the whole, then, it seems feasible to assert that one of the important ingredients in the popularity of history in the eighteenth century is the fact that it was a species of literature, a humane study, an art rather than a science.

In the *second* place, it will be readily admitted that the leading feature of the eighteenth century in the field of literature was its keenness and alertness in the matter of expression. It was an age in which the form counted as much as the matter of thought—probably even more ; and all who aimed at literary renown paid the utmost attention to stylistic perfection. Like good workmen, they never submitted their manuscripts to the printer without first subjecting them to a scrutiny and emendation almost incredible in its persistency and extent. Hence an eighteenth century book is generally an object of pure delight to the eye, apart altogether from the pleasure it gives to the mind ; its punctuation is no less commendable than its observance of all the stylistic proprieties of the age. Sometimes, as in Gibbon's case, the testing and trying to which the text was submitted were mental, and therefore previous to the actual writing ; [1] in other cases, notably Hume's, the eye was summoned to aid the ear, and the text was laboured with numberless corrections, almost all verbal, both in the manuscript and afterwards when it appeared in print.[2] It was not a matter, be it observed, merely of finding the exact word, and of stitching the sentences together in such a way as to make the transitions easy : the architecture of paragraphs, and indeed of whole chapters, was seriously considered, in order that the emphasis might be properly controlled and

---

[1] *Autobiog.*, p. 201.

[2] Burton, II, pp. 279-80 : " His manuscripts . . . were subjected to a painful revisal. We sometimes find him, after he has adopted a form of expression, scoring it out and substituting another ; but again, on a comparison of their mutual merits, restoring the rejected form, and perhaps again discarding it when he has lighted on a happier allocation of words " ; cf. also *Ibid.*, pp. 142-3.

justly distributed, the shades of meaning duly brought out, and the details grouped artistically. So widespread was this vigilance in composition that it would be invidious to distinguish between the greatest writers : all who reached to any perfection in the art—scientists, philosophers, historians—took for their motto Quintilian's injunction, " *Vigilandum ducat, interum enitendum, pallendum.*" [1] Particularly noteworthy is the fact that the most memorable pronouncement of the period on style fell from the lips, not of a professed literary critic, but of a scientist—Buffon. In his celebrated address to the French Academy, on the occasion of his reception, occurs this striking passage : [2] " Well-written books alone will pass on to posterity. The quantity of information, the singularity of facts, even the novelty of discoveries, are not sure guarantees of immortality. . . . These things are outside the man : style is the man himself. . . . If the works which contain them (i.e. information, facts, discoveries) turn only on small concerns, if they are written without taste and without genius, they will perish."

Clearly it was no mere itching after fine effects that produced the constant laudation of taste in the eighteenth century : the entire culture of the age lay behind it. In France, thanks to the influence of the Academy, the movement which had begun in the previous century for the purification of the language had resulted in the establishment of a sound literary currency of great purity and strength. No word or phrase was permitted of an *outré* character, that savoured of barbarism or pedantry, that overtaxed or put a strain upon the intelligence of the average cultured person—the *honnête homme.* " *L'honnête homme,*" said Descartes, " *n'a pas besoin d'avoir lu tous les livres, ni d'avoir appris soigneusement tout ce qu'on enseigne dans les écoles.*" [3] All that was required for the comprehension of even the most profound of books, provided the author discharged his task satisfactorily, was

[1] *De Institutione Oratoriâ*, lib. VII, Cap. X, quoted in Maury, *Œuvres Choisies* (1827), I, p. 354, note.
[2] Buffon : *Œuvres Choisies*, ed. Hémon, pp. 480-1.
[3] Taine : *Ancien Régime*, p. 242 ; Descartes : *Recherche de la Vérité*.

common sense (*le bon sens naturel*).   In the *salons*,[1] where the
ideals of the age found their most acute expression, savants
were placed upon trial by an alert, select, and mundane
society, measured by a yardstick that had, as a rule, nothing
to do with their respective spheres of investigation, and
applauded or condemned according as they succeeded or
failed in assimilating their specialized knowledge to the
general body of intelligence possessed by their hearers.[2]
"I compare the eighteenth century," said M. Taine, "to a
society of people who are at table ; it is not sufficient that the
food prepared and presented to them should be easy to take
and digest ; it must also be a dish, or better still, a dainty.
The mind is an epicure."   In such circumstances, tediousness,
diffuseness, dull erudition were unpardonable ; it was impossible for the man of learning to plead the exigencies of his
subject, and escape into the obscurities of a jargon : he must
render himself comprehensible and agreeable, or be relegated
to outer darkness.   In short, he must show *goût, grâce,
esprit, élégance, lumière, bienséance, justesse,* and many other
kindred qualities in his conversation.   All this, of course,
reflected itself in the literary style of the period, and, in
particular, in the style of historians ; for it was impossible
that there should be two languages—one for the study and
the other for society.   Hence a celebrated critic once remarked
that literature in the eighteenth century was "one long
conversation."

It is easy to point out the defects of so drastic a system.
For one thing, it tended to throw discredit on erudition as
such, and to put a premium on the facile pen and the shallow
discursive brain.   Nevertheless the advantages were considerable.   Men of letters were humanized by dipping in
the common platter.   Ceasing to be pedagogical or merely
informative, they strove to be interesting without losing
accuracy, to be perspicuous without becoming naïve, to be
piquant, witty, epigrammatic, and ironical without sacrificing

---

[1] Roustan : *Les Philosophes et la Société Française au XVIIIe Siècle*—
" Être lancé par un salon constitue, à cette époque, le moyen le plus sûr
d'arriver ; le salon est aux réputations naissantes et même nées ce que la
presse est de nos jours " (pp. 203-4).
    Taine, p. 336.

scholarship. Sensibly or insensibly they imparted to the most recalcitrant matter the grace and charm commonly associated only with the most airy and frivolous of subjects.[1]

But if the cult of literary expression was carried to a high pitch of perfection in France, France had not a monopoly of the art : she was simply its supreme exemplar. From one end of Europe to the other the French language, French ideals, French manners and customs spread like a contagion from the *foyer* of Paris, creating a community of culture such as the world had not seen since the days of the Roman Empire. " An opinion launched from Paris," said Joseph de Maistre,[2] " is like a battering-ram propelled by thirty millions of men." Even England, in spite of her strongly insular tradition, did not escape the effects of this Gallican intellectual supremacy. Writers like Pope, Addison, and Johnson, however much they differed among themselves as to the hall-mark of good literature, were united in the emphasis they laid on taste, propriety, dignity, perspicuity, wit, congruity of ideas, justness of conception, and the other qualities that dominated literature across the Channel. " True wit," sang Pope,[3] " is nature *to advantage dress'd*." " The taste of our English poets," wrote Addison, " is extremely *Gothic*." And Johnson instructs [4] the poet not to number the " streaks of the tulip," but to exhibit, in his portrait of nature, " such prominent and striking features as recall the original to *every mind*." It was not an accidental characteristic of the period, therefore, that English writers who aimed at carving out a niche for themselves in the temple of fame, desired above all things that their works might be translated into French and win the applause of the *salon*.

The *third* ingredient in the popularity of history in the eighteenth century was its intimate association with philosophy. All the literary historians of the period contrived to

---

[1] Roustan, p. 208.
[2] Sorel : *L'Europe et la Revolution Française*, I, p. 150 ; also pp. 151-5— "Il n'y a plus aujourd'hui de Français, d'allemands. . . . " Quoique l'on dise ; il n'y a que des Européens."—Rousseau, *Sur le Gouvernement de Polagne*.
[3] *Spectator* : " True and False Wit," May 11, 1711.
[4] *Rasselas*, Chap. X.

regard their subjects as, in some sene, an *addendum* to philosophy, an extension of the philosophic mind backward, as it were, into the past. This extension, moreover, was perfectly normal and natural at the time ; for the philosophers of the Age of Reason, being lineal descendants of Locke,[1] were entirely empirical in their attitude to truth : that is, they based their systems on the ascertained facts of experience and shunned whatever savoured of mysticism, or could not be demonstrated by the ordinary processes of reasoning.[2] To such thinkers history was a veritable godsend. Where was there to be found so rich a repertory of reliable truth about humanity as the documents of history could afford, if only they were properly handled. With the record of the past at their disposal, the philosophers felt they could erect a building four-square to all the winds of criticism that nothing could overturn. And contrawise, just as they turned to history to provide them with *data*, so also they illumined their history by the aid of their philosophy and impressed upon it a meaning and a value which it never before possessed. History for history's sake was a formula which they would not have accepted, had it been put to them. On the contrary, they would have said something like this : " By all means let us have history, but let it prove something, let it take us somewhere, let it provide us with a view of the world and human life." The person who set out to record past events for the sole purpose of displaying them, as they really were, would have struck them as a species of pedant, a pedlar in detail, an antiquary, a man without culture and without taste. But observe the consequences of this attitude so far as the general reader is concerned. There is nothing so instructive and entertaining as the interpretation of facts by means of a theory. If it is well done, as men like Voltaire and Hume could do it, it is irresistible, overwhelming, and

---

[1] Hibben : *The Philosophy of the Enlightenment*, Chaps. I and X. Leslie Stephen : *English Thought in the XVIIIth Century*, I, p. 94.
[2] " I banish all hypotheses from my philosophy."—Toland : *English Thought*, I, p. 106. " We must therefore glean up our experiments in this science from a cautious observation of human life, and take them as they appear in the common course of the world, by men's behaviour in company, in affairs, and in their pleasures."—Hume : *A Treatise of Human Nature*, Introduction.

entirely satisfactory to the mind, exactly as a puzzle properly worked out is satisfactory. Nothing remains when the task has been completed, save to applaud the brilliant executant. Let it be frankly admitted : the bulk of general readers do not want to know the facts in themselves : they want to be saved the troublesome task of thinking ; and the author who sorts them out in clear, logical sequence, uses them dexterously to prove something, supplies clues galore, will always command a large and sympathetic audience. While the industrious individual who laboriously strives after factual accuracy, and subordinates everything else to this prime consideration, who perhaps loses symmetry in his anxiety to state all the relevant facts, and often forgets style in his anxiety not to be guilty of an over-statement, this individual will find his book labelled by the *vulgus profanum* as academic, pedantic, and dull. So it was, at any rate, in the eighteenth century. The man with a " philosophy " was on top, the industrious labourer in the mine of historic fact was pushed into a second or even a third place ; and history was devoured primarily because it was entertaining and instructive and amusing. In other words, the core of an historical work was the doctrine it contained.

§ 3

IT is important, then, if our object be to understand the ideas that animated Voltaire and his " school," to relate them to their philosophical environment, that is, to the movement known as the " *Enlightenment.*" [1] The source of this curious phase of thought which dominated Europe during the eighteenth century is generally traced to the great advances made by Science in the latter part of the seventeenth. Step by step, under the impulse communicated by Bacon and Descartes, investigations based upon the experimental method of reasoning had pressed back the

[1] The bulk of the matter in this section is derived from Leslie Stephen, *English Thought in the XVIIIth Century*, Vol. I ; and Taine, *Ancien Régime*, p. 223 sqq.

frontiers of the unknown, and built up an impressive structure of demonstrable truth concerning both the organic and the inorganic worlds. The fruitful principle from which this extension of knowledge proceeded was the permanence and inflexibility of natural law. To the scientist, nature appeared in the light of a gigantic mechanical contrivance, operated by a connected and coherent system of " springs and balances," whose purpose and function it was possible to discover by patient research. It was an easy step from this assumption about nature to the general position that man, hitherto an anomaly in the scheme of things, must also fall within the scope of the same laws : he was part of the natural world, and, as such, must be subject to its economy. And from this, again, it followed that all man's activities—intellectual, moral, religious, political, economic—ought to be susceptible to scientific treatment, and become intelligible on this basis, like the natural order. In other words, what Descartes held out as a possibility in his *Discours,*[1] and Fontenelle, the most famous of his disciples, actually believed,[2] seemed about to become, when the Age of Reason dawned, the working faith of the intellectual world. The task of the eighteenth century was to apply the experimental and inductive method, by which Science was achieving its conquests, to ethics, politics, religion, and economics ; in a word, to complete the subjugation of all cosmic phenomena to the mind of man.

If the seventeenth century supplied the eighteenth with its method of investigation, it also provided it with its concrete problems. At the same time as science was making its wonderful advances, there was taking place, mainly as the result of these advances, a revolutionary change in the whole setting and circumstance of human life. Thanks to geographical progress, the old mediaeval conception of a world bounded by the frontiers of Christendom, with its bright edges rimmed in the darkness of nations whose exis-

---

[1] *Discours,* Seconde Partie—" Ces longues châines de raisons, toutes simples et faciles, dont les géometres ont coutume de se servir pour parvenir à leurs plus difficiles demonstrations, m'avaient donné occasion de m'imaginer que toutes les choses qui peuvent tomber sous les connaisances des hommes s'entresuivent de mêmes."

[2] Brunetière : *Ét. des Critiques,* Vol. VII, p. 243.

tence was relatively of no account, had crumbled to pieces before the awe-inspiring spectacle of an earth peopled by millions, the vast bulk of whom had never heard of the Christian faith ; and by civilizations far more ancient and august than that of Europe. And where geography ended astronomy took up the tale. Newton removed the veil from the heavens, revealing for the first time the depths of inter-stellar space ; and out of his epoch-making discoveries came a new map of the universe, relegating the earth and its inhabi-tants to a relatively insignificant position on the fringes of an apparently boundless Cosmos. "Through the roof of the little theatre," says Sir Leslie Stephen,[1] " on which the drama of man's history had been enacted, men began to see the eternal stars shining in silent contempt upon their petty imaginings." " *Voilà l'univers si grand*," exclaims Fon-tenelle's Marquise,[2] " *que je m'y perds ! Je ne sais plus où je suis ; je ne suis plus rien : la terre est si effroyablement petite !* " The exclamation is symbolic of the intellectual crisis provoked by so stupendous a revelation, and the difficulty experienced by the mind in accommodating itself to the new conceptions of time and space. But, as was perhaps inevitable, it was religion that suffered the greatest shock. How could the accepted ecclesiastical explanation of man's destiny be fitted into the new framework constructed by the geographers and astronomers ? Was the God of Christianity the same as the God evolved by the scientist from the order and mechanical perfection of the universe ? Or had the stage become too vast for the drama portrayed in Scripture ? If so, a fresh interpretation of the Christian faith, or, at all events, a revaluation of the old beliefs was imperative. Here, then, we have an indication of the type of problem the eighteenth century found incumbent upon it to solve and elucidate. But the religious difficulty was only the most spectacular of a whole congeries of difficulties knocking at the door of the human mind for solution. Every aspect of intellectual activity had to be reviewed in the new light, and the necessary adjustments made, in order to bring theory into line with the realities discovered by the scientist.

[1] *English Thought*, I, p. 82.   [2] *Pluralité des mondes*.

Being an " Age of Reason," the eighteenth century went to
work coolly and rationally, convinced that the instrument it
wielded was capable of unlocking all secrets and dissolving
all mists.

With the manifold controversies occasioned by the attempts
of thinkers to carve a path for themselves through the débris
of old and moribund metaphysics we need not concern ourselves ; they belong rather to the domain of the philosopher
than of the historian, who is interested primarily in objective
results.   But it is important for us to realize the influence of
the great dispute, in preparing the way for the new historiography.

In England, the most prominent feature of the *Enlightenment* was the appearance of Deism.[1]   As its name implies,
this was an attempt to lay down the principles of a universal
religion of reason, by discovering the elements common to
all religions.   There is no difference, said the deist, between
morality and religion : the essence of the one consists in acting
according to the nature of things as reason has disclosed it ;
the essence of the other in acting according to the nature of
things as God has revealed it.   Strip religion of the supernatural and mysterious envelope in which it is wrapped up,
and the real substance which lies at the heart of it, its *raison
d'être*, so to speak, will be found to be simply a moral code.
That the supernatural and mysterious could be thus removed
without weakening the sanctions of religion was, in the
opinion of the deists, a supreme test of the value of any
creed.   Thus the justification of moral action lies in the fact,
not that God has commanded it, but that reason has demonstrated it to be consonant, with nature.   " Obey nature,"
became their watchword, " and you cannot disobey God." [2]

It was to be expected, of course, that so bold an application
of scientific analysis to a subject hitherto hedged off from
interference by the ordinary processes of reasoning would
at once raise an outcry.   The deists were condemned by
the orthodox theologians as atheists in disguise.   But
the peculiarity of the situation in England was that the

---

[1] *English Thought*, I, Chaps. II, III, IV.
[2] *Ibid.*, I, pp. 139, 144.

exponents of the Christian faith met the onslaught half-way.[1] Instead of using their privileged position as officers in the State Church to crush the deist by sheer force, they grappled with his arguments, and rationalized theology as far as they safely dared. Christianity, they argued, is perfectly compatible with the religion of reason ; the Christian God, however darkly we may perceive Him, is none other than the God of nature. In the long run, thanks to superior scholarship and sounder learning, they won their case. But the penalty was heavy : they had compromised with rationalism and opened the door to a continuous infiltration of the rationalist spirit into the Church. " It was often difficult," remarks Sir Leslie Stephen " to distinguish a rationalizing theologian from an out-and-out rationalist." Many a defender of orthodoxy, who imagined he was fighting a battle for spiritual religion, was really more of a danger to his own friends than to the enemy. Moreover, the spiritual temperature of society suffered, in the process, a considerable setback.[2] The unreality of the whole debate, the freedom of utterance on both sides, the acrid character of the arguments advanced —all this reacted very unfavourably on the position accorded to the Church by the " world." It became the fashion with the cultured classes to profess indifference to religion ; and the pulpit, afraid to be charged with either superstition or fanaticism—the twin enemies of reason—confined itself to moral platitudes, backed by commonsense appeals to the facts of life." In short, it must have seemed as if Bossuet's prophecy was realized, and protestantism had ended in scepticism.

In France a different development took place. There the rationalizing tendency of the age was opposed by a stiff, unbending orthodoxy, which, instead of seeking compromise, resorted to the mediaeval weapon of persecution, imprisonment, and exile. Consequently the French *Enlightenment* was marked by violence and extravagance of every description. Iconoclasm was the order of the day. Thinker after thinker hurled himself with volcanic energy against the established strongholds of obscurantism and superstition.

[1] *English Thought*, I, p. 169.   [2] *Ibid.*, pp. 272-3.

Nothing was too sacred or ancient to escape criticism, nothing too complicated or mysterious to defy analysis ; like rays of light, to which they were frequently compared, the shafts of reason penetrated everywhere.   Sacrilegious hands were laid on beliefs that the Christian world had hitherto accepted as literally and completely as the diurnal course of nature. Prescriptive rights were invaded with a recklessness that shocked the conservative and the timorous.   Destruction, in fact, followed in the footsteps of the army of reason as closely as its shadow.   But the *philosophes* did not trouble with the casualties they inflicted on the empire of unreason ; their one aim was to emancipate mankind from the fetters of authority and tradition.   High in the heavens the sun of reason illuminated the human mind like a second revelation, the infallible solvent for all problems, the sure guide for erring humanity through the labyrinth of the world.   " *La seule manière d'empêcher les hommes d'être absurdes,*" wrote Voltaire, " *c'est de les éclairer* " ; [1] and again, " *La vertue quand elle est éclairée, change en paradis l'enfer de ce monde.*" [2]

There is clearly something intolerant and at the same time amusing in this crusade of the French *philosophes*.   M. Taine compares [3] them to Puritans or Mohammedans—that is, to fanatics.   And though the comparison seems a trifle far-fetched, the imputation it conveys is not unjust ; they were actuated by a dogmatic belief that the age in which they lived marked so stupendous an advance upon the past [4] as to throw into the shade all previous achievements of mankind since the collapse of ancient civilization.   Hence the past was regarded in the light of a bondage to be escaped from, rather than a heritage to be enjoyed.   Hence the impatience and contempt with which they looked back on the toilsome ascent of the race from savagery to "civility."   How slowly

---

[1] *Remarques de l'Essai,* 1763.
[2] Voltaire à M. le Chevalier de Richelieu, 20 Sept., 1760.
[3] *Ancien Régime.*
[4] " This progress," comments Croce, " is, so to speak, a progress without development, manifesting itself chiefly as a sigh of satisfaction and security as of one favoured by fortune, who has successfully encountered many obstacles, and now looks serenely upon the present," etc.   *On History,* p. 244. Un citoyen de Paris se promenait dans cette grande ville avec plus de luxe que les primiers triomphateurs romains n'allaient autrefois au Capitol.— Voltaire, *Siècle de Louis XIV*, Chap. XXIX.

humanity marches, exclaimed Voltaire, towards wisdom!
Hence, also, the prolific use of the word "Gothic" as
equivalent to "barbaric," and the confident assumption
that the standard of taste and civilization attained in the
eighteenth century was a fit and proper criterion for the
judgment of all ages. Even Thomas Wharton, the learned
author of the *History of English Poetry*, moderate as he was,
colours his work with the prevailing prejudice; showing
that England as well as France shared in the general attitude
of the *Enlightenment* towards the past. "We look back," he
writes,[1] "on the savage condition of our ancestors with the
triumph of superiority; we are pleased to mark the steps by
which we have been raised from rudeness to elegance, and our
reflections on the subject are accompanied with the *conscious
pride* arising, in a great measure, from a tacit comparison of
the *infinite disproportion between the feeble efforts of remote
ages and our present superiority in knowledge*."

[1] *History of English Poetry*, Preface.

VOLTAIRE

CRITICAL estimates of Voltaire's work have been written from many angles, and the most diverse judgments have been passed upon it. This is perhaps unavoidable in the case of one who touched contemporary life at so many points, wrote voluminously on topics of public interest, and was himself a kind of epitome of an entire century. In the following pages we are concerned only with a fragment of the man—that part which reveals itself in his histories. But it is well to remember, at the outset, the amazingly rich and varied genius with whom we have to do. " In whatever branch of literature one practises," remarks Condorcet,[1] "that person will always have an immense advantage, who has an extensive or profound vision in another." So, at any rate, it was with Voltaire. He was an acknowledged master of literary expression, one of the greatest of *grands écrivains* : a thinker who amassed probably more accurate information about the world in all its aspects than any man since Aristotle ; and, above all, one who possessed a remarkable capacity for collecting, condensing, simplifying, and re-directing the scattered lights shed by all manner of studies on the problems arising out of human existence. " As a simplifier and populariser," says M. Taine,[2] " he had no rival in the world." If, in addition, it be also borne in mind that this same mercurial genius moved about among men, grappled with affairs, was consulted and almost worshipped by most of the crowned heads of Europe, it will be apparent how eminently fitted he was for the task of writing humanely and attractively on history. It was virtually impossible for one so gifted by nature, and so conversant with the political and intellectual currents of the age, to take up the pen of the historian and fail to be interesting. One thing his temperament forbade him to become—a pedant.

[1] *Vie de Voltaire: Œuvres,* I, p. 214.   [2] *Ancien Régime,* p. 343.

In all his utterances, whatever the subject might be, he preserved the freshness, unconventionality, and vigour of the man who infallibly rises superior to the matter in hand. Historians may regret that he did not document his statements, that he paid little or no deference to the courtesies of the profession, that he never by any chance displayed the scaffolding by which his conclusions were reached ; but the plain truth is, that to demand such things of him would be to presuppose a Voltaire very different from the Voltaire of history. In all matters he was a law unto himself—a Melchizedec of the historical priesthood ; and as such he must be allowed to create the taste by which he is judged. The vigour and velocity of his style, the impatience with which he overrode the mechanical and formal aspect of learning, and the transparent sincerity of his mind were all wrapped up together as part and parcel of his unique genius. To ask that he should be like other men is to ask the impossible.

The career of Voltaire as a historian is soon told. He made his *début* in 1731 with the *History of Charles XII*. Then followed a silence of some twenty years, during which he occupied himself with poetry and natural philosophy. But the continuity of his interest in history is shown by his *Letters on the English*, and by the assiduity with which he immersed himself in historical studies of all kinds. It was, in fact, the seed-time preparatory to the wonderful harvest of his maturity. During these years his ideas, reduced to paper before they were ripe, were frequently handed about among friends and disciples, purloined, garbled, and published by piratical booksellers, who doubtless thought to profit by the distinguished name of the author. Strickly speaking, it was not until after 1744, when he was appointed historiographer of France, that he seriously set about the task of placing his views *in extenso* before the public. In 1751 began the succession of brilliant histories which established his fame and spread his name throughout Europe as the greatest of living historians : the *Siècle de Louis XIV* (1751), the *Annales de l'Empire Depuis Charlemagne* (1753), the *Essai sur les Mœurs et l'esprit des Nations* (1756), the *Histoire de l'Empire de Russie sous Pierre le Grand* (1759), the *Prècis du Siécle de*

Louis XV (1769), and the *Histoire du Parlement de Paris* (1769).

Of all these works three stand out prominent—the *Siècle*, the *Essai*, and *Charles XII* ; the others, readable as they are, must be regarded as of inferior merit, and more or less negligible in any attempt to reconstruct his historical outlook, his method, and his teaching. But it should be noted that, along with the three full-dress histories, account must be taken of the many letters, remarks, sketches, essays, observations, and criticisms which he showered from his pen, either as prefaces or *addenda* to his historical works, or as independent writings, justificatory of his standpoint and of the judgments he passed on history. Before any complete account can be given of his historiography, it is necessary to group, classify, and arrange these occasional discussions ; for they embody the doctrine of which his histories are merely the exemplification. We shall have to quote from them frequently ; and if our excursions take us further afield, the references will be given in the foot-notes.

HIS CONCEPTION OF HISTORY

It is generally assumed that Voltaire's intellectual father in the subject of history was the English statesman, philosopher, and dilletante—Bolingbroke.[1] When the latter gave currency to the now familiar aphorism, " History is philosophy teaching by examples," he sounded a note that found a ready echo in the mind of his brilliant pupil. At first sight, indeed, it might appear as if the views of the two men were identical. Both, for example, shared the same contempt for the " learned lumber " of the antiquary ; both insisted that historical learning (and indeed learning of all kinds) is not an end in itself, but a means to an end ; and both claimed that history, properly understood, is a school to train men in virtue and citizenship. Possibly Voltaire laid more stress on the purely literary aspect of the subject than

---

[1] Voltaire's debt to Bolingbroke is not clear. Fueter (p. 349) thinks the interchange of ideas was *oral* only—" mündliche Gedankenaustausch." Julleville, *Histoire de la Langue et de la Littérature Française* (Vol. VI, p. 94) asserts that, after Bayle, Bolingbroke was Voltaire's chief teacher.

Bolingbroke. " I have a queer idea in my mind," he once remarked ; [1] " it is only those who have written tragedies, who are able to infuse interest into our history. . . . A history like a drama, ought to have *une exposition, un nœud, un dénouement.*" But, in the main, his chief concern, like Bolingbroke's, was to rescue history from the dead hand of the antiquary, and to make it cultural, utilitarian, and didactic. [2]

The instruction which history, written in this way, might convey was both comprehensive and varied. The body of fact set forth by the historian might be made the basis of generalizations and precepts useful in handling the problems of the day ; or, by suggesting comparisons of present conditions with those prevailing elsewhere or at other times, it might inspire contentment or emulation ; or, again, by placing before men's eyes the record of crime and folly which comprises the bulk of history it might prevent them from repeating the errors and disasters of their ancestors. In every case the effect on those who laid the teaching to heart would be a more thoughtful and active participation in the political and social life of their own day.

The lessons of history, moreover, were not only for the citizen : they had their interest and value for the monarch. In Voltaire's opinion, there was no mentor to be compared with the unbiased written record ; for, in history, men, however exalted, receive their deserts : the evil they do lives after them, the good is *not* interred with their bones. Seated on high, like a dispenser of divine justice, the historian by his pen dooms the bad to everlasting shame, and elects the good to perpetual and honourable remembrance.[3] " There is no sovereign," he remarks in his Preface to *Charles XII*,[4] " who, in reading the life of this monarch, ought not to be cured of

---

[1] Voltaire à d'Argenson, 26 Jan., 1740 ; also Voltaire à Schouvalow, 17 Juli, 1758 ; and Voltaire à Marmontel, 11 Avril, 1772—" Je dis qu'un homme qui écrit bien une fable en écrira beaucoup mieux l'histoire."

[2] The didactic note, however, was not to be too pronounced : " Il faut écrire l'histoire en philosophe, mais qu'il ne faut pas l'écrire en précepteur, et qu'un historien doit instruire le genre humain *sans faire le pédagogue.*"— Voltaire à Thieriot, 31 Oct., 1738.

[3] " Le jugement de la posterité est le seul rempart qu'un ait contre la tyrannie heureuse."—" Essai sur les Mœurs," Chap. CLXVI.

[4] *Œuvres*, XVI, p. 133.

the folly of conquests. If any prince or minister find disagreeable truths in this book, let them remember that being public men, they owe an account of their actions to the public . . . that history is a witness and not a flatterer ; and that the sole means of compelling men to speak well of us is to do good."

In all this one detects the peculiarly optimistic and delusive belief of the age, that enlightened reason is the sovereign instrument for remedying the ills of humanity. Men are everywhere the same, was the argument ; therefore give reason a chance, set it face to face with the *tableau* of history, let it assimilate the principles embodied in this *tableau*, and inevitably it will proceed to institute a more rational order.[1] On the other hand, deny men the instruction history affords, and the flood-gates will remain open for a return of the devastating tide of fanaticism, madness, and violence, which deluged society in the ages of unreason. " *Anéantissez l'étude de l'histoire, vous verrez peut-être des St. Barthélemy en France et des Comwells en Angleterre.*"

But if the full import of Voltaire's conception of history as an instructor is to be understood, a wider sweep is necessary. At the beginning of his remarks prefatory to the *Essai sur les Mœurs et l'esprit des Nations* he explains how he came to break away from the practice of historians in his day. His friend, hostess, and correspondent, the Marquise du Châtelet, a celebrated blue-stocking of the period, had declared that the old-fashioned annalistic writers disgusted her by their inanities. Lack of perspective in their narratives, their inability to distinguish the actual conditions of the times they described, their fantastic pictures of barbarian leaders and mediaeval churchmen as if they were the equals of Cæsar and Scipio, their fabulous credulity, their tiresome repetition of trivial detail, their blind acquiescence in the Biblical tradition that the fortunes of the Jews formed the central point in the world's history ; and, withal, their ignorance of the process by which the peoples of Europe

---

[1] " Enfin les hommes s'éclairent un peu par ce tableau de leurs malheurs et de leurs sottises. Les sociétés parviennent avec le temps à rectifier leurs idées ; les hommes apprennent à penser."—*Remarques de l'Essai : Œuvres* XXIV, p. 548.

emerged from barbarism to " civility," their stupid silence on
such matters as the growth of laws, governments, institutions,
manners and customs, ideas—all this, in the opinion of the
Marquise, lowered history to the level of an insipid, futile
chronicle devoid of interest to the serious student.[1] It was
against such a method of writing history that Voltaire, with
the encouragement of the Marquise, set up a new conception
that can only be called revolutionary. He believed that
history, reduced to its simplest terms, is neither more nor
less than a record of ideas, or, as he would say, of *opinion* ;
that the *événements* with which historians had hitherto occupied
themselves—wars, party struggles, persecutions, Church
councils, revolutions, and diplomacy—were merely the outward and visible expression of the ideas current during an
epoch. " Ideas," he said, " have changed the world " ; all
else is subsidiary ; therefore let us study the growth of ideas.
And again, " My principal object, is to know, so far as
I can, the manners of peoples, and to study the human mind ;
I shall regard the order of succession of kings and chronology
as my guides, but not as the object of my work." [2] In short,
he was a student of the intellectual aspect of history.

One is tempted, at this point, to make a comparison
between the change effected in historical writing by Voltaire's
insistence upon intellectual values and the materialist theory
popularized by Marx in the nineteenth century. No doubt
the results are, in a sense, incommensurable ; but in each
case the innovation consisted essentially of a change in
standpoint. To Marx the motive force shaping the course
of history is economic ; the relation in which men stand to
each other as agents in production determines the whole
cultural, political, and ethical superstructure of a period.
To Voltaire the controlling force is intellectual ; and the
conditions prevailing at any time are the outcome of ideas
operating through individuals, classes, and institutions,
which are themselves the expression of these ideas. To
Marx, again, the gist of historical development consists in
class struggles for power—struggles in which those who

---

[1] *Remarques de l'Essai, Œuvres* XXIV, pp. 543-4.
[2] *Introduction à l'Abrégé de l'histoire universelle, Œuvres* XXIV, p. 51.

" have " oppress those who " have not," and are themselves
subjected, in the course of time, to the same fate. To
Voltaire the main thread of history is a warfare, in which men
endeavour to impose their own ideas, errors, and prejudices
on others, in order to dominate them ; only to be themselves
similarly victimized by fortune in the future. " We see in
history thus conceived," he wrote,[1] " errors and prejudices
succeed each other in turn and expel truth and reason. We
see the clever and the fortunate enslave the foolish and the
unfortunate ; and again, the clever and fortunate become the
playthings of fortune, like the classes they rule."

Clearly there is not a very great difference between these
two points of view, when we place them in a proper perspective, and consider the theories of causation they imply.
The Marxian conception is simply an application, from the
economic standpoint, of the doctrine which Voltaire had
already worked out on a purely intellectual plane.

But no special significance need be attached to this comparison ; Voltaire would not have understood the materialist
interpretation of history even if it had been explained to him.
It required the Industrial Revolution to bring it to the light.
He visualized history as the clash of ideas and the progressive
expansion of the human mind through the triumph of reason.
His picture of the main trend of European history from the
beginning of the Christian era, succinctly put, would be something like this : First of all, Christianity destroyed the
religions of the Ancient World and broke the peace which
humanity had enjoyed under the easy toleration of Rome ;
then it gave birth to the Mediaeval State and the Mediaeval
Papacy, two warring principles which plunged Europe into a
blood-bath for a thousand years. In the meantime, however,
while these antagonistic powers struggled for the mastery,
Mohammedanism annihilated Christianity in the East and
Africa, thereby becoming a menace to Christendom—a menace
which could only be met by war ; hence the Crusades, and a
further plunge into bloodshed. Then, again, when the
Mediaeval Church became corrupt, the Reformation split up the
unity of Christendom, severed many countries from the Roman

[1] *Remarques de l'Essai, Œuvres* XXIV, p. 548.

communion, and created sectarian strife, which plagued the world until the emergence of the sovereign State and the dawn of reason. Briefly, " it is the power of opinion, true or false, sacred or profane, which has filled the earth with bloodshed during so many centuries." [1]

Coupled with this predilection for " intellectual history " is to be reckoned Voltaire's interest in, and defence of, social as opposed to political history. He quarrelled with his courtly predecessors, because they not only missed the inner meaning of the events they narrated, but also because, like the despots who figured in their books, they sacrificed the human race to the exaltation of one man. [2] Grovelling, servile, lying, glorifying fraud and injustice under the guise of magnanimous actions, incapable of directing a fearless look at kings and priests, they seemed to him to avert their gaze from mankind to the comparatively worthless deeds of those whom the world accounted great. [3] But no history worthy of the name could be written with such a theme for its object. The motto ought to be *Homo sum humani nil a me alienum puto.* [4] What was wanted, in other words, was a history of humanity, that is, a reasoned account of the progress of society ; and although in this record the doings of kings must perforce figure, the foreground would be reserved for the truly great, those, namely, who have done good to their fellows. " What I should like to know," he writes, [5] " is the sort of society then in existence, how men lived in the interior of their families, what arts were practised ; " and again, " Just as it is necessary to know the great actions of kings who have changed the face of the earth, and especially those who have improved the condition of their peoples, so also we ought to ignore the vulgar crowd of kings who would only serve to burden the memory." [6] The test of progress, and the purpose of government, according to Voltaire, was the happiness of nations and states (*le bien-*

---

[1] *Remarques*, passim : Faguet, *Voltaire (Dix-huitième Siècle)*, pp. 224-5.
[2] *Introduction à l'Abrégé*, p. 51 : Voltaire à Vernet, 1 Juin, 1774.
[3] " Telle est la misérable faiblesse des hommes, qu'ils regardent avec admiration ceux qui ont fait du mal d'une manière brillante, et qu'ils parle-ront plus volontiers du destructeur d'un empire que de celui qui l'a fondé."— *Discours sur l'histoire de Charles XII, Œuvres* XVI, p. 130.
[4] *Nouvelles Considérations sur l'histoire, Œuvres,* XVI, p. 140.
[5] *Essai sur les Mœurs*, Chap. XII, p. 53.
[6] *Introduction à l'Abrégé*, p. 52.

être chez les hommes, le bonheur des États). This, of course,
included peace, security, good laws, sound finance, and the
spread of material well-being throughout the community ;
but it also included, in a pre-eminent degree, the cultivation
of the arts and sciences, education, enlightenment, *politesse*.
He waxes lyrical when speaking of the achievements of human
genius, the fadeless grandeur of the arts, the impressive
structures raised by science ; he would build altars to the
inventors of the plough, the weaver's shuttle, the carpenter's
plane, and the saw.[1] " A lock on a canal joining two seas,"
he remarks,[2] " a picture by Poussin, a good tragedy, the
discovery of a truth, are things a thousand times more precious
than all the narratives of campaigns." Hence the delight
with which Voltaire seizes upon those periods in history
when the human race enjoyed the fruits of its own unimpeded
genius—the Rome of Augustus, the Italy of the de Medicis,
the reign of Louis XIV. Hence also his dislike of " Gothic "
or barbarous ages, when the mind of man stagnated in
ignorance, and superstition flourished.

HIS IDEA OF CAUSATION

Assuming, then, that the goal of the historian is to describe
the progress of society, we may go on, in the next place, to
inquire how far, and in what ways, this progress has been
influenced, i.e. stimulated, retarded, or thwarted, by causes
which are capable of being ascertained by the human mind.
In other words, some principle, or principles, of causation
must be invoked if a reasoned narrative is to be built up out
of the vast mass of *data* confronting the historian. It is on
this point, perhaps, that Voltaire, in spite of his brilliance,
is somewhat disappointing ; he is neither consistent nor
profound. Rich enough in suggestions, explanations, and
generalizations, he undoubtedly succeeds in throwing a flood
of light over the entire field of history ; but his readers will
search in vain for anything resembling a unified conception

---

[1] " Thomas et Bonaventure ont des autels, et ceux qui ont inventé la
charrue, la navette, le rabot, et la scie sont inconnus."—L'A,B,C, *Œuvres*,
XXVII, p. 365.
[2] Hémon : *Cours de Littérature* (Voltaire), pp. 14-15.

of causation, which will carry them through the labyrinth, or enable them to grasp the meaning of events as a whole. On the contrary, his most ambitious work, the *Essai sur les Mœurs*, which is an attempt at a philosophical history of the kind he advocated, gives one the impression, as a French critic has remarked,[1] of *un joli chaos*, a tumultuous disorder, lacking design and direction. It is at once a sketch of manners, a record of political events, and a collection of amusing anecdotes ; but when we close the book and reconsider the general drift of the narrative, we are conscious of no central idea, no coherence, no unity.[2] As a history of Europe from Charlemagne to the Renaissance it is good—Robertson who traversed the same ground thought it surprisingly good ; but as an exemplification of Voltaire's own views on history it must be described as only a qualified success.

Nevertheless, it is possible, allowing for the tendency of Voltaire to vary his standpoint and to employ different methods of interpretation, to construct from his various writings something approaching a philosophical theory of causation, and to illustrate it with a fair degree of accuracy. To begin with, he was a Deist ; that is, he postulated the existence of a mechanical universe, operated by inflexible laws. " All beings," he said, " are subject to invariable laws." The evidence of design in Nature allowed him no other tenable hypothesis. Consequently he repudiated as an absurdity the providential, miracle-working Deity of the popular imagination. " The vulgar imagine God to be a king Who holds His seat of justice in His Court. Tender hearts represent Him as a father Who takes care of His children. But the wise man attributes to Him no human affection."[3] " I am not an atheist," he would say, " nor a superstitious person :[4] I stand for common sense and the golden mean. I believe in God—not the God of the mystics and the theologians, but the God of Nature, the great

[1] Faguet : *Dix-huitième Siècle.*
[2] Le livre fermé, cherchez à en retrouver ou rétablir la ligne générale et le dessein ! "—Faguet, pp. 278-9.
[3] Dict., art. *Homme* ; also art. *Miracles.*
[4] " J'ai vu la necessité de bien faire connaître ma façon de penser, qui n'est ni d'un superstitieux, ni d'un athée."—Voltaire à Cideville, Avril 12, 1756.

geometrician, the architect of the Universe, the prime mover, unalterable, transcendental, everlasting." But this God is a God outside the machine—He is a passive and spectacular Deity ; and it is a folly to connect Him directly with anything that happens on this insignificant planet. He is merely the constructor of the machine, Who has created it and set it in motion ; the machine itself runs its course according to the laws appointed for it, and nothing can make it diverge a hairs-breadth from these laws.

The existence of evil in the world is, of course, deplorable. Voltaire did not minimize the suffering of mankind—physical, intellectual, or moral—whether self-inflicted or contingent upon causes over which the individual has no control ; to him, as to Schopenhauer, it was stark, overwhelming, and unrelieved in its extent and acuteness, and pressed like a nightmare on his imagination which nothing could assuage. " The globe on which we live," he once said,[1] " is one vast scene of carnage and destruction," and human history is, for the most part, given over to " tigers " and " monkeys." In fact, we may close the book of nature and of man with the sigh :

> " O triste Muse de l'histoire
> " Ne grave plus à la mémoire
> " Ce qui doive périr à jamais." [2]

We may even wish to consign the whole record to the flames, as an insult to the reasonable soul of man.[3] But the wise man will not burk the grim reality ; nor will he gloss it over, like Leibnitz, with the formula, " the best of all possible worlds ; " [4] nor, again, will he try by casuistry or metaphysic to explain it away. On the contrary, he will accept it, as he accepts the earthquake and the thunderstorm, that is, as

---

[1] Dict., arts. *Puissance, Toute Puissance.*
[2] *Ode sur le passé et la présent* (1775), *Œuvres* VIII, p. 496.
[3] " O mon Dieu ! Si tu descendais toi-même sur la terre, si tu me commandais de croire ce tissue de meurtres, de vols, d'assassinats, d'incestes, commis par ton ordre et en ton non, je te dirais : Non, ta sainteté ne veut que j'acquiesce à ces choses horribles qui t'outragent," etc.—" Sermon des Cinquante."
[4] *Vide* " Candide " ; cf. also " The ' all is for the best ' of Shaftesbury, Bolingbroke, and Pope, is nothing but the effusion of a mind devoted to eccentricity and paradox ; in short, nothing but a dull jest."—Dict., art. *Puissance.*

part of the working of the machine. He will remember that all machines are imperfect, wasteful, and accompanied by jars, and shocks, and disturbances. Above all he will save the majesty and dignity of God by keeping Him rigidly out of the account, and by clinging to the only valid assumption, viz. that whatever may occur in the world, law is the necessary basis of things.

If, then, the universe is built on orderly lines, human history must embody the principle of cause and effect. It cannot be otherwise, since every man acts, and must act, according to the laws governing his being. Voltaire has no doubt at all on this point. In his view every event, from the bow of a dancing master, or the fall of a sparrow, to the collapse of an empire, is the product of the whole cosmic order ; and men and things are dragged along by a chain of cause and effect as helplessly as the waves and sands are driven by the winds.[1] In the light of so sweeping a statement, which, incidentally is a verbal translation of one of Voltaire's own sayings, it might seem as if we were justified in asserting that he was an out-and-out determinist in history. But such is not the case. His general theory is greatly modified when he comes to apply it to facts. For instance, he allows for the operation of chance, or fortune, in the ordering of human affairs ; so much so, indeed, that it is fashionable with critics [2] to ascribe to him a positive delight in tracking down the trivial occurrences that produce mighty results. As an instance of this sort of thing we might take the well-known incident, related by Voltaire in the *Siècle de Louis XIV*,[3] concerning the quarrel between the Duchess of Marlborough and Mrs. Masham, in Queen Anne's boudoir. Bolingbroke was the original author of the story. The Duchess—so runs the tale—upset a glass of water over the dress of her rival, Mrs. Masham, in the presence of the Queen ; as a result, she fell into disgrace, the Whigs fell from power, and the Tories coming into office changed the whole international situation by concluding peace with France at Utrecht. *Ergo :* a glass of water was the cause of the Treaty

[1] *Essai*, Chap. CXCVI. [2] E.g. Faguet : *Dix-Huitième Siècle.*
[3] Chap. XXII.

of Utrecht ! Other instances of a similar kind could be
quoted to the same effect. But it would be wrong to place
much stress on this aspect of Voltaire's historical philosophy.
Those writers who, on the strength of it, go to the extreme of
declaring that, in Voltaire's eyes, all history is a series of
fortuitous occurrences, are just as wide of the mark as those
who imagine that he was an inflexible determinist. We do
not conclude from the incident of the handkerchief in *Othello*
that Shakespeare believed human life to be the sport of
chance ; no more, it would seem, ought we to tax Voltaire
with so fatuous a theory, especially in view of the strong case
he puts forward on behalf of determinism. On the whole,
his attitude seems to be, that although the high gods may
appear to play [1] with human beings like wanton boys, the
so-called operations of chance, if we thoroughly understood
them, would be seen to be nothing but the necessary connexion
of all events in the universe. [2] But, having regard to our
imperfect knowledge, and the impossibility of ascertaining
the ultimate causes of things, it is perfectly right and proper
to describe certain events in history as due to chance.

Then, again, in spite of his determinism, he is not prepared
to assert that every event in history is necessarily an integral
part of an inflexible chain. Apart altogether from the
vagaries due to chance there are, he observes, loose ends and
inconsequences, things indifferent, as it were, in the general
scheme of things, which exercise no influence whatever on the
trend of history. " It is with the chain of events," he
remarks, [3] " as it is with a genealogical tree, where we perceive
branches that become extinct at the first generation, and
others that continue the race. Many events are without
filiation." If, for example, the cæsarean operation had not
been performed on Cæsar's mother, Cæsar would not have
overthrown the Republic ; or if Maximilian of Bavaria had
not married the heiress of Burgundy and the Netherlands,
Europe would have been spared two hundred years of war.
But whether Cæsar " spat to the right or to the left," and

[1] La destinée se joue de l'univers "(*Remarques de l'Essai*, 1763, *Œuvres*
XXIV, p. 561).
[2] *Essai*, Chap. CXXIV.
[3] Notes *sur le désastre de Lisbonne*, *Œuvres* IX, p. 472.

whether the heiress of Burgundy arranged her hair "this way or that "—these are clearly matters of no significance in the grand totality which we call history.[1] Now Voltaire uses this distinction between filiated and non-filiated events as a means of deciding what ought to be included and what ought to be excluded from historical disquisitions. He will not, for instance, tell us anything concerning the personal habits, accomplishments, or features of his chief characters, unless and until they impinge upon, and influence, the outer world, and thereby assume historical significance. Thus Colbert, Louis XIV's finance minister, is described by Voltaire as having *les sourcils épais et joints, la physionomie rude et basse, l'abord glaçant*—these physical characteristics express his personality as it touched other men, and therefore have a value in history ; but " how we were his neck-tie," being a matter void of political significance, and therefore beneath the notice of a serious historian, is left unsaid.[2] There is nothing new in this conception of the filiation and non-filiation of events ; every historian is perpetually confronted with the problem of deciding between the relevant and the irrelevant in the facts he handles, and he acts pretty much in the way Voltaire describes. But in the eighteenth century it was necessary to issue a warning, because history proper had not completely separated itself off from the chronicle ; and the bane of the chronicle was inconsequence and irrelevance. Everything was grist to the mill of the chronicler—plagues, famines, pestilences, eclipses, miraculous occurrences, monstrosities, etc.—not because they bore any historical value in themselves, but because they had taken place, or were said to have taken place.[3] Hence it must be conceded that Voltaire did a good deal towards elevating history from an inconsequential chronicle to something approaching a scientific analysis of events.

Besides the two modifications of the general determinist position to which allusion has just been made Voltaire is compelled to admit a third. He does not banish freedom from the world of human action. Freewill, in the sense of

[1] Notes *sur le désastre de Lisbonne*, *Œuvres IX*, p. 472.
[2] *Siècle—Supplément, deuxième partie*, *Œuvres XV*, p. 123.
[3] Cf. Mezerai, *Histoire de France*, passim.

willing without a cause, he asserts, is a contradiction in terms :
no man is free in that sense. The will is determined by the
nature of things. But, although the will is not free, the
individual is free, so long as he possesses the power to act in
accordance with what he wills. Only the person who is
debarred from carrying out what he desires to do is unfree.[1]
The distinction is, perhaps, a commonplace, but it is of great
importance in Voltaire's historical philosophy ; in fact, from
it depends his entire conception of the driving force in history.
Men, he would say, have made the world what it is, not
Providence ; and history is a purely secular process, the result
of individual and communal passions working themselves
out, consciously or unconsciously, in a series of movements,
sometimes violently, sometimes more peacefully, but always
accompanied by some disturbance and destructiveness. Of
all the passions, the most radical is self-love, which is the
basis of self-preservation. But, by a perfectly comprehensible process, this necessary and, up to a point, beneficent
quality becomes transmuted into selfishness or self-interest,
that is, into a settled principle of action, or attitude to life ;
and finally it manifests itself as arrogance, ambition, love of
fame, lust for power, and the desire to dominate others. It
is, moreover, intolerant by nature, and seeks to achieve its
ends by violence or deceit. In the former case it leads to
wars, assassinations, murders ; in the latter it is disguised
under the sacred name of diplomacy. But whatever form it
may assume, and whatever means it may employ, it is potentially the greatest destructive force in the world ; and if it
enjoyed complete freedom of action, would lead to the
sabotage of society.

Fortunately mankind is not without the means of arresting
and making good the devastation it brings in its course.
Side by side with self-love Voltaire discovers, embedded, as
it were, in the tissue of the human brain, the germs of something better and higher—the instinct for justice,[2] and the
love of order. He is careful to explain that these are not

---

[1] Dict., arts. *Destin, Liberté.*
[2] " Il n'y aurait eu aucune société, si les hommes n'avaient conçu l'idée
de quelque justice."—*Philosophe Ignorant*, 31-8.

"innate ideas," which Locke had exploded long before ; they evolve, it would appear, with the growth of the mind, and, in this sense, are as much a part of man's nature as the brute passions. Their function is to rescue, adjust, and construct. " In the midst of these plunderings and destructions which we observe during the space of nine hundred years," writes Voltaire,[1] " we see a *love of order* which secretly inspires the human race, and has prevented its total ruin." Slowly but surely this latent energy of the race repairs the chaos wrought by ambition, arrogance, and the lust for power, creates the conditions of progress, and carries mankind forward.[2]

Furthermore, from time to time there arise great men, who gather up and incarnate in themselves the spirit of epochs ; and through them the constructive power of humanity finds its best and most salutary expression. They are the *demiurges de l'humanité*, the true heroes of the race—Cæsar, Charlemagne, Alfred, Alexander III, St. Louis, Columbus, Henry IV, Peter the Great, Frederick, Louis XIV, etc. The test of their greatness is the measure of good they confer upon the world.

Thus history is to be viewed as a struggle of rival and opposing forces, a record of passion, folly, and crime, lit up and traversed periodically by human genius. In other words, there is intelligence presiding over the movements of society ; but it is not the intelligence of Bossuet's supernatural Being : it is a plural intelligence with its seat on the earth. To the old historical monotheism has succeeded a historical polytheism.[3] The idea is possibly a trifle shallow, possibly no explanation at all to the modern mind. But in the eighteenth century it heralded a revolution in the writing of history. Nor can it be denied that by transferring the direction of events from a mystical incomprehensible Deity, to the shoulders of humanity itself, Voltaire opened the way for a more rigorous and scientific investigation of the laws of progress. The theory of natural causation, which he pro-

[1] *Essai*, Chap. XCVII.
[2] " L'industrie des hommes a été beaucoup plus loin encore que leur fureur." —*Essai*, Chap. CXCVII.
[3] Faguet : *Dix-huitième Siècle.*

pounded and worked out, is the groundwork of modern historical research. We stand upon the vantage ground his genius work won from the obscurantist and the dogmatist.

So far it would seem as if Voltaire's idea of history may be reduced to a very simple formula. He pictures it as a battle, in which the forces of destruction associated with man's passion of self-love in its numerous manifestations contend for the mastery with constructive forces proceeding from the primary instinct of justice : a battle, moreover, which always ends, however long the struggle may be, in the progressive triumph of order, reason, and civilization. But Voltaire does not leave us to grope about in this abstract and nebulous realm of warring principles for a concrete solution of the complexities of history. In the *Essai* he descends to earth and announces a theory of causation, which has, at all events, the merit of being tangible. " Three things," he says,[1] " influence the mind of man incessantly, climate, government, and religion : this is the only way to explain the enigma of the world."

It was not until Bodin published his *Méthode Historique* and *République* in the latter part of the sixteenth century that the influence of climate began to be appreciated as a means of interpreting the facts of human history.[2] As in the case with all new departments of inquiry, it remained largely speculative and theoretical until the basis of fact on which it rested became sufficiently extended and rationalized to warrant scientific deductions. But the conception was seductive ; and there was a strong tendency—not so much in Bodin's case [3] as on the part of his successors—to press matters to an extreme, and to claim for the theory an absolute validity. Thus while Montesquieu undoubtedly enriched history by his celebrated analysis of climatic influences in the *Esprit des Lois,* he exaggerated greatly when he expressed the view that against material factors morality was practically powerless.[4] It was really a question of balance : whether,

---

[1] *Essai*, Chap. CXCVII.   [2] Baudrillart : *Bodin et son Temps*, Chap. XV.
[3] " Le climat a sur l'état des âmes une grande puissance sans doute, mais non par absolue."—Baudrillart, p. 151.
[4] *Ibid.*, p. 417.

on the one hand, the conscious intellectual and moral activities
of man were to be regarded as merely the consequence of
material conditions, or, on the other, these conditions, however potent, were to be treated as subsidiary to the main
ideological development. To ignore environment was to
fall into the Scylla of an absurd mysticism ; to ignore the
spiritual factor, was to drive straight into the Charybdis of a
crude materialism.[1] With his usual good sense and penetration Voltaire set himself to strip the theory of its glamour and
to give it the place due to it, and nothing more. Broadly
speaking, he was opposed, on principle, to any mechanical
interpretation of history that conflicted with the freedom of
man to determine his own destiny, or to any reading of the
facts that threatened to destroy the fundamental unity and
uniformity of human nature and human action ; he would
admit no factors that could not be resolved in some way or
other into conscious motives, or, as he would say, "moral
causes." But within the limits of this conception he was
prepared to give climate its place as a potent influence.[2]
"The sun and the atmosphere," he says, "mark their empire
on all the productions of nature from man to mushrooms."
Thus, climate may determine the strength and beauty of the
human body, our inclinations, and also the character of our
genius, together with the outward or ceremonial part of
religion. Equatorial races are black or brown, those of
temperate regions are fair : Lapland does not produce a
Hercules, nor Africa a Newton ; the Hindu bathes ceremoni-
ously in the Ganges, and the Arab refrains from pork—all
these and many other historical facts are susceptible of
geographical or climatic interpretations. But, if climate
is "everything," asks Voltaire, "how can we explain the
vicissitudes of Egyptian, Greek, or Roman civilizations :
all of which are now sunk in torpor ? Obviously the clue
is not to be found in climate. Again, it would be a fallacy
to assert that the northern races have always vanquished the
southern, or that religious doctrines apply only within certain
geographical limits ; the conquests of the Arabs, and the

[1] Baudrillart, p. 415.
[2] *Dict.*, art. *Climat* ; *Essai*, Chap. CXCVII ; Dict., art. *Lois (Esprit de)* ;
Commentaire sur l'Esprit des Lois, Œuvres XXX, pp. 442·5.

spread of Christianity are proofs to the contrary. Likewise with regard to Montesquieu's contention that the spirit of liberty dwells exclusively in *mountainous* regions : if so, how may we explain the rise of the Dutch, Venetian, and Polish republics ? " There is no end to the wealth of illustration with which Voltaire combats the view that history is the handmaiden to geography. From the tenth to the sixteenth century Italy passed through a wonderful series of revolutions ; but " the Apennines are still in the same place, and the Po has not changed its course." In the Middle Ages the same brutal fanaticism, the same frauds of priests, the same ambition of princes, prevailed throughout the length and breadth of Europe—in the " Hycanian forest," on the " banks of the Thames," and among the " orange groves " of Naples—geography notwithstanding. The English beheaded Mary Stuart and Charles I " without inquiring whether the wind blew from the north or the south " ; Conradin and Frederick of Austria suffered the same fate " in the bright sunshine " of Naples. Clearly, he concludes, it is not heat and cold, humidity and dryness, that decides the fate of the " miserable mortals who crawl, suffer, and reason on this globe " ; the dominant influences are government and religion.[1]

On the subject of government Voltaire discourses with all the prejudice and conviction of his class and age. Politically, he was an aristocratic republican, that is, he would have preferred to see the government in the hands of the enlightened classes. But he lived in a Europe ruled by despots, and accepted the system as he found it. Moreover, he had nothing but praise for the benevolent ruler—*un véritablement bon roi est le plus beau présent que le ciel puisse faire à la terre.*[2] He looked to governments to secure and extend the principle of toleration, to hold in check the fanatical propensities of the *canaille*, to widen the area of enlightenment by wise laws, to develop education, to foster the progress of the arts and sciences, and to liberate the energy of human genius in every direction. Like the encyclopædists, he had a remarkable

[1] *Commentaire sur l'Esprit des Lois, Œuvres* XXX, pp. 405-64.
[2] *Ibid.*, 455 ; *Pensées sur le gouvernement, Œuvres* XXIII, p. 533.

confidence in the potency of good legislation ;[1] wherever he
meets with it in history his praise is unstinted. But Voltaire
had no illusions on the score of what governments can do.
At best they are only means to an end, and frequently they
are very defective means. " Laws," he says,[2] " have proceeded in almost every state from the interests of the legislators, from the exigency of the moment, from ignorance, and
from superstition, just in the same manner as cities have been
built." It is within their power to create the conditions
out of which true freedom arises ; but freedom itself consists
in the emancipation of the mind from error and prejudice—
plus les hommes seront éclairés, plus ils seront libres. To the
historian, the state of the laws and the form of government
under which a people live are mainly useful as indices of the
level of civilization attained at any period. Hence the care
with which Voltaire analyses the various types of administration, law, and policy he encounters in his historical
excursions, and the stress which he lays on custom, the
offspring of law.

But when all allowances have been made for the operation
of climate and government in the shaping of human affairs,
the chief place, he says, must be given to religion. Here,
again, Voltaire was the child of his time. Like all the
philosophes, he showed great bitterness and uncompromising
hostility to organized religion ; only, in the violence of his
epithets he probably surpassed every one. His attitude
might be described as a compound of fiery intolerance of
clerical oppression and an equally fiery conviction that
religion and morality are necessarily one and the same thing.[3]
The cardinal point on which his attitude rests is that all
religions transcending the purely savage conception of God
as an object of terror,[4] are equally grounded on the universal
and elementary moral needs of mankind, and teach the same
truths. *Adore moi et sois juste !* [5] is the behest of the Deity,

---

[1] Fueter, p. 352.
[2] *Dict.*, art. *Lois*, §1: "Les lois de toute espèce, qui sont la medicine des âmes, ont donc été composées presque partout par des charlatans, qui ont donné des palliatifs, et quelques-uns même ont presenté des poisons."— *Pyrrhonisme de l'histoire*, Chap. XXXVIII.
[3] Morley : *Voltaire*, pp. 175-6. [4] *Dict.*, art. *Dieu.*
[5] *Profession de foi des Théistes*, *Œuvres* XXVII, p. 56.

whether it is spoken by the mouth of Zoroaster, Confucius, or Jesus. From which it follows that the entire human race stands united upon a common acceptance of "natural religion." *La religion,* he states, *enseigne toujours la même chose à tous les peuples sans aucune exception ;* and, again, *la morale inspire partout la concorde.*[1]

In history, however, no positive religion is to be found, which embodies pure theism and pure morality, except, possibly the early cult of the Chinese.[2] As a general rule, all manner of corruptions, accretions, and superstructures, have been added to the plain, unvarnished truth by ingenious and ambitious men, for their own selfish ends ; with the result that what was intended to be the great binding and remedial force in the world has become the prime source of its destruction, devastation, and death. Dogmas make their appearance—*le dogme alors est la trompette qui sonne la charge* [3]—priests usurp power by means of these dogmas, over the credulous and ignorant, mysterious rites are invented to strengthen the illusion, sects divide over incomprehensible shibboleths, popes amass power by the help of false documents and attempt to dominate States ; while men, enveloped in clouds of sophistry, absurdity, and error, lend themselves willing tools to intolerance, persecution, burnings, and murders, in the sacred name of religion.[4] In brief, a Hell upon earth is the dire result of depressing moral truth and placing dogma in the foreground as the essence of religious belief.[5] "Theology," he remarks, "has never served any other purpose than to upset men's minds, and sometimes states. From Calchas to Gregory VII . . . the power of priests has been fatal to the world." [6]

For Judaism, the cradle of Christianity, he has nothing but vituperation.[7] It is the religion of a *chétive* nation, *un*

[1] *Essai,* Chap. CXCVII ; *Dict.,* art. *Théisme.*
[2] " Il n'y a eu qu'une seule religion dans le monde qui n'ait pas été souillée par le fanatisme, c'est celle des lettrés de la Chine."—*Dict.,* art. *Fanatisme.*
[3] *Remarques de l'Essai*, *Œuvres* XXIV, p. 553.
[4] *De la Paix Perpétuelle,* § XXXI ; *Essai,* Chap. LXII.
[5] " L'autorité a voulu ordonner aux hommes d'être croyants au lieu de leur commander simplement d'être justes."—*Remarques de l'Essai,* p. 573.
[6] *Dialogues entre A. B. C.,* Xme entretien ; *Dict.,* arts. *Prêtres, Lois* § iii.
[7] *Essai,* Chap. VI ; *Phil. de l'hist.,* Chap. XLII ; *Dernières Rémarques sur Pascal, Œuvres* XXXI, p. 36.

peuple brigand, atroce, abominable, whose law is the law of savages, whose history is a tissue of crimes committed against humanity.   There is, in fact, no more barbarous religion in the world.   Ignorant, avaricious, superstitious, carnal, blood-thirsty, fanatical, and exclusive, the Jews, in Voltaire's eyes, outshine all the peoples of antiquity in pride, arrogance, and intolerance.   They know neither hospitality nor liberality ; they murder their masters when they are slaves, and never pardon when they are prosperous.   " Cringing in misfortune, indolent in prosperity," they are the " enemy of the human race."

Thus the obvious conclusion to be drawn from Voltaire's analysis of the part played by religion in history is, that it has barbarized the world.   One is reminded of the immortal epigram, attributed to Gibbon, " I have described the triumph of barbarism and religion." [1]   But the argument put forward by Voltaire is ludicrously unfair.   It is perhaps true that if all men accepted a pure theistic creed, together with the simple moral code based upon it, they would not quarrel about dogmas, or persecute, or wage religious wars.   But what justification is there for the contention that the elimination of dogma would end wars and persecutions ?   Assuredly the struggle for the possession of the earth would still go on, economic and political rivalries would still be rife, and national interests would still collide, whether there were dogmas or no dogmas to fight about.   If Voltaire had not been infatuated with a theory he must have seen that intolerance is not a creation of religion ; it is latent in human nature.   Men will always be intolerant of opposition, and attempt to crush their enemies whenever they have the opportunity.   Even in pagan antiquity, which Voltaire, in common with Gibbon, so much admired :   Socrates was put to death because he dared to question the religious beliefs of his time.   And Voltaire himself was not long dead when his own countrymen haled the aristocrats to the guillotine, because they stood for a different political *régime* from that demanded by the majority.

[1] *Vide* p. 170.

VOLTAIRE AS A HISTORICAL CRITIC

Generally speaking, we should expect that the man who is instrumental in creating a new type of history will also have something to say about the technical aspect of his work. It can hardly be otherwise ; for every historian must procure and handle his material according to some principle or principles which commend themselves to his reason ; and if his conception of what ought to form the substance of history differs greatly from that held by other workers in the same field, it is practically certain that his idea as to what constitutes a correct historical method will also be very different. As soon as Voltaire set about the illustration of his ideas on history, he became, of necessity, involved in the problem of method ; and just as he found himself in sharp opposition to the conception of historical composition prevalent in France before his day, so also he became a rebel against the existing practices of researchers. According to Voltaire, the outstanding weakness ot previous historical books lay in the thoroughly unsound and unscientific method employed by their writers in handling *data* : they failed to discriminate clearly between the true and the fabulous. All other departments of secular knowledge had yielded, or were yielding, to the inroads of the scientific spirit ; history alone remained the stronghold of credulity, obscurantism, and tradition. The consequence was that the record of the past was encumbered and distorted by all manner of absurdities such as only immature minds could be expected to swallow. " The majority of historians," he remarks,[1] " instead of discussing facts with men, tell stories to children." This defect, he thought, could only be remedied by importing a healthy scepticism into history, or *pyrrhonisme*, which would draw a meridian line once for all between the provinces of fable and history proper. The idea was, like all Voltaire's ideas, derivative : it had been announced by Bayle before him ; but no one could have applied it with so much vigour and common sense as Voltaire. To begin with, he laid down as a

[1] *Rémarques sur l'histoire, Œuvres* XVI, p. 136.

base line, the general definition that history is the recital of
facts represented as true : fable, the recital of facts represented as fiction.[1]   But he is careful to point out that even
after we have established the separation, and winnowed away
the chaff of myth from the wheat of historical truth, the
residuum must not be regarded as " fact " in the scientific
sense :   that is, demonstrable certainty ;[2] for there is no
certainty, says Voltaire, except when it is physically or morally
impossible that the thing can be otherwise—a condition that
cannot be established with regard to any historical event.
Moreover the multiplicity of " witnesses " makes no difference ;
the depositions of even 12,000 men amount only to a probability.[3]   In the days before Copernicus, mankind was
" certain " that the sun rose and set ; but their certainty was
an error for all that.[4]   And so it must be in history : for
even under the most favourable conditions " all the great
events of this globe are like the globe itself, one half
of which is in brilliant light, and the other plunged in
obscurity." [5]

On this assumption, then, that history is not, and cannot
be, an exact science, Voltaire lays down certain rules whereby
the truth, within the limits prescribed, may be discovered,
and error avoided.   The first is, that nothing contradictory
to the regular course of nature should be believed.   Let us
refuse credit, he says, to any historian, ancient or modern,
who reports things contrary to nature [6]—*ce qui n'est pas dans
la nature n'est jamais vrai*.   Further, whatever appears to
clash with common sense or strike the mind as miraculous,
monstrous, or exceptional, must be treated as improbable
unless the weight of evidence is overwhelming.   In such
cases it is important to have comparative information to go
upon.   For example, it would be difficult, he asserts,[7] to
reconcile the sublime ideas held by the Brahmins concerning
the Supreme Being, with their superstitions and fabulous

[1] *Dict.*, art. *Histoire.*   [2] *Dict.*, art. *Certitude.*
[3] *Dict.*, art. *Vérité.*   [4] *Dict.*, art. *Certitude.*
[5] *Pyrrhonisme de l'histoire*, Chap. XVII.
[6] " Refusons notre créance à tout historien ancien et moderne qui nous
rapporte des choses contraires à la nature et à la trempe du cœur humain."—
Préface to *Charles XII.*
[7] *Essai*, Chap. III.

mythology, if history did not show us parallel contradictions among the Greeks and Romans.

Again, the reliability of witnesses is a matter to which the most careful attention must be paid. The Whigs, says Voltaire, condemn the Tories for betraying England, and the Tories allege that the Whigs sacrificed England to their own interests ; how then shall we ascertain the truth in the matter ? If both are to be believed, obviously there is not a single honourable man in the nation. In such a case, the only course for the historian is to accept as true the facts admitted by both ; these are indubitably true ; on the other hand, whenever there is contradiction, doubt must supervene, and the historian must suspend judgment. The same rule applies, of course, to all Memoirs written by men who took part in the events they describe, e.g. Clarendon, Ludlow, Burnet, De Retz, La Rochefoucauld, etc.[1] It is particularly applicable when it is a question of determining the rights and wrongs in a quarrel between crowned heads ; in this case, the difficulties are increased because of the numerous agencies that exist for obscuring the issue and making the worse appear the better reason.[2] As for the evidence of obscure persons in obscure places, it is historically valueless ; so also are all dates and events for which no evidence of observation can be adduced. Finally, it is always advisable, he asserts, to be exceedingly sceptical as to the evidence derived from " monuments " and " festivals." We are naturally inclined to imagine that a monument, raised by a nation in celebration of a particular event, would attest the certainty of that event ; but if it is not erected by contemporaries, or if it commemorates an event which carries little probability, it can only be regarded as proving the existence of a wish to consecrate a popular opinion.[3] At best, such evidence merely testifies that those who originally built the monument or invented the festival, believed that they stood for facts. " In general," he writes,[4] " be sure when you see an old

---

[1] *Dict.*, art. *Certitude de l'histoire.*   [2] *Essai.*
[3] *Dict.*, art. *Histoire.*
[4] *Essai*, Chap. XXIV : " Une fable a quelque cours dans une génération ; elle s'établit dans la seconde ; elle devient respectable dans la troisième ; la quatrième lui élève des temples."—Cited Buckle, II, p. 313, note.

festival, or an antique temple, they are the works of error ; this error gains credence after two or three centuries ; finally, it becomes consecrated, and temples are erected to chimæras."

Closely allied to the *mensonges* of history, in Voltaire's view, are to be reckoned "portraits" and "anecdotes." He objects to the anecdote [1] because it is usually made to minister to the debased craving of the multitude for information about the *vie intime* of celebrated personages ; in addition, it is derogatory to the dignity of history, whose motto should be "tell posterity nothing but what is worthy of posterity." If it be objected that the historian ought to conceal nothing, Voltaire's reply is, that the fact or facts in question must have some bearing on public events, if they are to be chronicled. His objection to portrait painting by historians was perhaps more deeply rooted. The anecdote might conceivably have an artistic value ; but the portrait seemed to him pure charlatanry. The reason for this antipathy is perfectly plain : it lies in his peculiar psychological tenets. "The soul," he asserts,[2] "is nothing but a continuous succession of ideas and sentiments which follow each other and are mutually destructive. . . . There are, of course, certain ideas and dominant passions, children of nature, education, and habit, which, in varying degree, accompany us to the tomb. But these leading traits of the mind are also subject to change every day, according as we have slept badly or suffered from indigestion. The *character of every man is a chaos, and the writer who seeks to disentangle this chaos, only creates another."* What then ? Must we conclude that it is impossible to depict character in history ? Not at all, says Voltaire, character can be depicted, but it must be by, and through, the objective acts of the individual. The historian must confine himself to the effects whch the individual's personality produces upon his environment, and from these build up his conception. Or, to quote Voltaire, *On ne peut appercevoir la caractère que des faits.*

The next important point after the determination of what

---

[1] *Preface, historique et critique.—Histoire de la Russie.*
[2] *Supplément au Siècle de Louis XIV*, Deuxième Partie, *Œuvres* XV, pp. 123-4.

constitutes the *data* of history, is the management and selection of the facts to be recorded. Here, Voltaire's antipathy to the otiose compilations of his predecessors, finds a congenial outlet. With a majestic wave of the hand, he bids the historian take a comprehensive view of his subject, focus on the great topics and personages, and allow the details to sink into their true proportion—and insignificance. To load the text with them is to obscure the meaning of what is truly significant, to encumber the march of the narrative, and to render history insipid and unreadable.[1] " Confound details," he exclaims ; [2] " they are a vermin which destroy books ; posterity forgets them all." And, again : details are the " impedimenta " of history, the " baggage " of the army.[3] The aim of the historian, as he conceived it, was not to trouble about the year in which one insignificant prince succeeded another in an obscure and barbarous age, and such like uninstructive information ; but " to fix men's minds on the striking revolutions of history which have changed the manners and laws of great States." [4] To this end it was necessary, he thought, to make a careful selection from the immense *recueils* of fact, and to leave the rest in their proper place, the public archives.[5] " If there were only one book in the world," comments Voltaire,[6] " children would know it by heart, all the syllables would be counted ; if there had been only one battle, the name of each soldier would be known and his genealogy would pass on to the remotest posterity ; but in all this long succession, almost uninterrupted, of bloody wars which christian princes wage with each other, the old interests, which have all changed, have been effaced by new ; the battles of twenty years ago are forgotten for those of our own day : just as in Paris the news of yesterday is obliterated by that of to-day, which, in its turn, will suffer the same fate to-morrow ; and almost all events are driven by each other into everlasting oblivion."

---

[1] Voltaire à Schouvalow, 14 Nov., 1761.
[2] Voltaire à l'abbé Dubos, Feb., 1738.
[3] *Phil. de l'hist.*, Chap. XIV.   [4] *Essai*, Avant-propos.
[5] " Les mémoires, les dupliques et les répliques, sont des monuments à conserver dans les archives . . . mais rien n'est plus insipide dans une histoire."—Voltaire à Schouvalow, 14 Nov., 1761.
[6] Preface, *Histoire de la Russie.*

TWO CONSEQUENCES

Several interesting consequences follow from Voltaire's conception of history and of the manner in which it ought to be written. If the first place, the assumption on which his criticism is based, viz. that human nature is the same all the world over, and that customs alone vary, leads to a curious sameness in his presentation of events. His characters move about in a world lacking atmosphere, or, rather, in a kind of tropical region, where distance and perspective are annihilated, and everything hurts the eye by its clearness. As the drama unfolds itself, dresses and manners change, the scenery shifts, the grouping of the actors varies, but there is no essential difference in the plot or the action. It is probably here that Voltaire presents his greatest divergence from the standards and ideals of to-day. It seems never to have crossed his mind that the mediaeval man, for instance, differs from the modern by the whole heaven ; not merely because his material environment was different, but also because the whole structure of his mind, the circle of ideas, beliefs, illusions, and prejudices, within which he lived is different. Yet, to bridge over this psychological gap, to recover the spirit of past epochs, to make Godfrey of Bouillon, Joan of Arc, and the other personages of mediaeval history more than mere puppets of the pen—this is the supreme task confronting the historian. And presumably the first step towards the goal is to divest oneself of prepossessions current in one's own age, to look for differences rather than similarities and to expect the strange and the unconventional.[1] But Voltaire was content, as indeed were all his contemporaries, to measure all ages against his own. If men acted differently or incomprehensibly in the past, they were either misguided, or imbeciles, or the story is a lie. The test of their significance is their intelligibility to an enlightened Frenchman of the eighteenth

[1] " I hold only that person really qualified and justified in taking up historical studies, who is in a position to adjust himself to each standpoint of the past, to experience over again every past spiritual experience of mankind, to think over again and feel the motives that give rise to its actions."—Maurenbrecher (Bernheim : *Lehrbuch*, p. 767).

century. Take, for example, his comment on the persecutions of Diocletian. " How could a man," says Voltaire,[1] " who was sufficient of a philosopher to abdicate the Empire be so little of a philosopher as to become a fanatical persecutor ? " It would be *un scandale de raison, par conséquent une improbabilité, par conséquent un mensonge* : and there is an end of it. Why trouble to search out differences when we know that there is nothing new under the sun ? Oracles in the ancient world, what were they ? They were simply an instance of the very human art of deception. Divination ? Simply an " invention of the first rogue who met a fool." Druids ? Merely " stupid impostors." King Pepin's Donation to the Pope ? No more valid, forsooth, than the gift of an island by Don Quixote to Sancho Panza.[2] As for the differences that divided Catholics and Protestants over the eucharist, during the doctrinal struggles of the Reformation, they are incomprehensible and absurd. The papists profess that they *eat God and not bread*, while the Lutherans *eat God and bread*, and the Calvinists *eat bread and not God*.[3] But it all comes to this, that " if anyone told us of a like extravagance and madness among Hottentots and Kaffirs, we should think we were being imposed upon."[4] How amusing again, was the claim of the reformers that they " opened the doors of the convents," when all they did was to " transform human society into one vast convent." [5] As for the execution of heretics in the Middle Ages, they are on a par with the slaughter in a Mexican temple. " If an asiatic had arrived at Madrid on the day of an *auto-da-fé*, he would not have known whether it was a merry-making, a religious festival, a sacrifice, or a massacre." [6] Or take the famous comment passed on the Norman Conquest of England. William defeats and kills Harold, and sends his captured banner, together with a share of the spoil, to the Pope : " but strip the transaction of accidentals," says Voltaire,[7] " and what does it become ? " Simply " the action of a Norman brigand

---

[1] Faguet, *Dix-huitième Siècle* ; *Essai*, Chap. VIII.
[2] *Pyrrhonisme de l'histoire*, Chap. XX.
[3] *Essai*, Chap. CXXVIII.   [4] *Profession de foi des Théistes.*
[5] *Essai*, Chap. CXXXIII.   [6] *Essai*, Chap. CXL.
      [7] *Essai*, Chap. XLII.

and a Lombard receiver of plunder." ." And this," he
remarks, " is at bottom what every usurpation reduces
itself to."

No doubt the rationalistic treatment _renders history
interesting ; it is not so obvious, however, that we are thereby
enabled to understand its meaning any better. What the
modern mind craves is not the reduction of all events and
characters to a common denominator, but their differentiation.
After all, there is a vast difference between the slaughter of
captives in a Mexican temple and the burning of heretics in
Europe, which no amount of ingenious comparison can possibly
conjure away. To compare them at all is to be guilty of the
most heinous sin a historian can commit—the sin of being
un-historical.

In the second place, the unconventionality of Voltaire's
conceptions led him to undertake a revaluation of previous
historical writings, it being manifestly impossible to define
a new attitude without working out its relations to that
hitherto assumed. This, moreover, is said to constitute his
greatest service to the cause of history. As a historian he is
probably to be ranked beneath the English triumvirate ; as
a critic he stands on a plane by himself, and the importance
of his conclusions is undeniable. The procedure he adopted
was both summary and to the point. Is the matter related
natural ? Is it probable ? Is it consonant with reason and
common sense ? Is the evidence adduced in support of it
sufficient in quantity and trustworthy in quality ? If not,
then it cannot be accepted : it is a *mensonge*, and those who
relate it as fact are really romancers. The sanctity of great
names did not trouble him : he pursued his way contemptuous
of tradition and authority. Take, for instance, his treatment
of early Roman history. It was customary for writers during
Voltaire's day, and previous to it, to copy and recopy uncritically the tales recounted in Roman historians concerning the
foundation of the city, as if Livy and the others were inspired
books. Tradition, it was said, had consecrated these tales,
and to question their authenticity was to shake the foundations on which history rested. Into this atmosphere of blind
credulity came Voltaire with the shattering announcement

that the first five hundred years of Roman history were neither more nor less than a tissue of fables—could not be otherwise, in fact, because no nation can possibly know its own origin. The art of writing comes late in the development of society, and, *a fortiori*, history which depends on the art of writing must come later still ; in short, it is the child of leisure, order, and civilization.[1] There was no gainsaying the force of the argument : if the early history of Rome was to be written, the first thing to be done was to discover the documents ; and if these were not to be found, a fresh start would have to be made from a totally different standpoint. Buckle's comment on the point is illuminating.[2] After examining Voltaire's remarks, he asserts that, in all essential respects, he anticipated Niebuhr, and thus became the herald of the nineteenth century movement, which resulted in the complete rewriting of the early period of Roman history.

But the dethronement of Livy as a credible historian was only one of Voltaire's achievements ; he carried his attack with the utmost nonchalance and boldness against the entire " field " of ancient historians. Under his severe scrutiny Tacitus becomes a clever satirist, depicting the decadence of Roman society against a mythical background of Germanic virtue ;[3] Plutarch a *récueil d'anecdotes plus agréables que certains* ;[4] Dion Cassius a calumniator, journalist and flatterer ;[5] Suetonius a retailer of hearsay ;[6] Herodotus the father of fables.[7] In fact, the only ancient historians who gain rather than lose in lustre at Voltaire's hands are Thucydides, Xenophon, and Polybius. The value of these judgments, however, is not that they would meet with the unqualified approval of modern critics—in the main, they do —but that they created, for the first time, a wide breach in the walls of tradition and opened the way for the entrance of the scientific spirit.

In regard to mediaeval history he speaks with much

[1] *Dict.*, arts. *Histoire, Préjugés.*
[2] *Hist. of Civilisation in England,* II, pp. 310-11.
[3] *Essai,* Avant-propos ; *Pyrrhonisme de l'hist.,* Chap. XII.
[4] *Siècle,* Chap. XXV.   [5] *Dict.,* art. *Cuissage ou Coulage.*
[6] *Extraits de la Gazette Littéraire,* VII.   [7] *Dict.,* art. *Diodore et Herodote.*

greater severity, but with considerably less success : partly because he suffered, like all writers of the eighteenth century, from an unconquerable disgust for its " Gothic barbarism," partly because he was not familiar to the same degree with its writers.   Nevertheless his views are worth noting for the light they throw on his general principles.   Broadly speaking, his criticism rests on the assumption that history is the product of an enlightened age.   The Middle Ages were barbarous and credulous ; consequently, the writers who flourished then cannot be expected to portray accurate pictures either of the past or of their own times.   Such chronicles as have come down to us are, in Voltaire's eyes, simply a mass of tiresome fables, painted against a background of superstition and fanaticism.   " Let us rank all the tales of Gregory of Tours," he exclaims, " with those of Herodotus and the *Arabian Nights* ! "[1]   A monkish chronicler tells us that Charles Martel defeated the Saracens in battle, or that Clotair II became insane : well and good ; he may be speaking the truth.   But when he goes on to say that Charles killed 360,000 Moslem, or that Clotair was afflicted with insanity because he stole an arm of the statue of St. Denis, and put it in his oratory, he is talking pure fiction.[2]   Things do not happen thus in history.   Or, coming to a later period, what trust is to be placed in the story of St. Bernard ?   One would have to be an idiot, remarks Voltaire, to believe that God performed miracles by the hand of this monk in order to assure the success of a crusade, when all the time its failure was due to bad leadership and faulty organization.   And so, he concludes, mediaeval history must remain in obscurity because there are no authentic documents to go on : *il faut le secours des archives et on n'en a point !* [3]   Comment on this mistaken judgment is probably superfluous ; but one naturally wonders what Voltaire would say if he were to revisit the earth and see the enormous advances made by mediaeval studies since his day.   From the much-despised monkish chronicle has been evolved a mass of information, in parts, no doubt, conjectural, but in the main as reliable as any

[1] *Pyrrhonisme de l'hist.*, Chap. XVIII.   [2] *Essai*, Introduction, Chap. LII.
[3] *Pyrrhonisme de l'hist.*, Chap. XI.

historical information can be. Indeed, the most striking thing about the mediaeval chronicle, when properly treated, is not its untrustworthiness, but its credibility.

To follow him in his perambulation through modern historical literature would entail a study in itself, and it would consist, largely, of a barren summary inferior to his own admirable *catalogue raisonnée* attached to the *Siècle*. It is important, however, to note the fact that he was by no means the iconoclast and contemner of his predecessors he is often imagined to be. On the contrary, his praise and blame are distributed with an even-handed justice, in strict accordance with the general credibility of the authors concerned. If they show evidence of a critical spirit he praises ; if they are credulous he condemns. He displays no bias against erudition as such, provided it is intelligently applied. Thus he admires Machiavelli, Guicciardini, and De Thou as the fathers of modern history[1]—the Thucydides, Xenophon, and Polybius of the modern world. He has nothing but eulogy for Ducange, Duchesne, and Baluze—they are worthy of " eternal gratitude " for their elaborate researches. Of the " profound " Mabillon, the " careful " Tillemont, and the " learned " Muratori the same might be said. But Père Daniel and Mezerai he finds " tiresome " : [2] the former, because of his predilection for military affairs, as if, for all the world, he were a *sarjent de bataille* instead of a Jesuit.[3] Bossuet again, is *illustre* ; but his history is false in spite of its elegance and force : " *il a menti*," says Voltaire,[4] " *avec une élégance et une force admirables*." Rapin, Rollin, and Dupleix are good ; [5] so also, it is pleasant to hear, are the English historians, Marsham, Hyde, and Sale.[6] But the Bollandists, with their *Vitæ Sanctorum* and *Acta Martyrum*, are despicable.[7]

---

[1] " On peut dire que jusqu' à Guichardin et Machiavel nous n'avons pas eu une histoire bien faite " (*Essai*, Chap. X) ; also *ibid.*, Chap. CXXI ; and Voltaire à Damilaville, 21 Mar., 1766.
[2] " Mezerai et Daniel m'ennuient " (Voltaire à d'Arginson, 26 Jan., 1740) ; also Catalogue, *Daniel*.
[3] Voltaire à Formont, 19 Juin, 1755.
[4] Voltaire à d'Olivet, 6 Jan., 1736 ; *vide* also pp. 72-3.
[5] *Siècle*, Catalogue.
[6] *Siècle*, Chap. XXXIV.
[7] *Essai*, Chap. IX.

THE THREE MASTERPIECES

There are many differences to be observed between the three most important of Voltaire's historical works—differences in character, scope, and treatment. *Charles XII* the most juvenile, and, in the opinion of at least one critic, the most perfect of all, gains its importance primarily, because it heralded the great historical heresy with which the name of Voltaire is associated, and provided French historians with their charter of emancipation. In contradistinction to the " classical school," who copied Livy and pursued their investigations " back to the Tower of Babel," Voltaire chose his topic from recent history, and threw overboard the customary paraphernalia of "harangues and portraits." The subject was not only selected from recent history : it was practically contemporary, for the exploits of the Swedish Napoleon still reverberated through Europe, like the rumbling of a thunderstorm which has passed beneath the horizon. No more arresting or romantic topic could have been chosen. But, apart from this, *Charles XII* differed from previous histories in its highly artistic conception and finish, and in its professedly didactic purpose. The dramatic and "moral" elements are supplied by representing the career of the hero as a struggle against fate, first as the favourite of Fortune, and latterly as her dupe. In fact, a good sub-title for the work might be some such phrase as *Les jeux de l'héroisme et de la Fortune*. In the early part of the narrative the star of the king is in the ascendant : he triumphs over Russia at Narva. In the second part, crossed by the rising star of Peter the Great, he buries his hopes and ambitions in the disastrous campaign ending in Pultawa, leaving

> A name at which the world grew pale,
> To point a moral and adorn a tale.

It is permissible, however, to doubt whether Voltaire made the most of his dramatic and didactic opportunities. As the Abbé de Mably pointed out,[1] " The author runs like a mad-

---

[1] *Manière d'écrire l'histoire*, (*Œuvres Complètes*, XII).

man in the wake of a madman " : there is lack of background and of contrast. Conceivably Voltaire might have written with greater effectiveness, both as a historian and a literary artist had he contrived to depict the exploits of his hero against the sombre stage of Sweden's sufferings, the progressive breakdown of the splendid monarchical edifice which Gustavus and Charles X had raised, and the general dislocation produced by a foreign policy out of touch with the actual needs and circumstances of the time. But of these matters there is little or no mention.[1] Yet the real tragedy of Charles XII's career surely lies, not in the fact that he was beaten by Fortune or by Nature, but by the logic of events. He was his own worst enemy. " The casualties of Fortune," remarks Montesquieu,[2] " are easily repaired ; but who can be guarded against events that incessantly arise from the nature of things ? " Charles, for all his military genius, was but a shoddy Alexander, who failed because he could not separate in his mind between the possible and the impossible : he pursued a chimæra. While he wandered in the deserts of Poland and the Ukraine, imagining himself to be master of the world, his crafty, resourceful, and patient enemy, making use of the experience he had gained at Narva, was steadily building up the power that was eventually to crush him. So far as Russia was concerned, Pultawa was simply the coping-stone to a policy based upon skill, prudence, and grasp of reality—in a word, a victory of *realpolitik* over romanticism. Thus, instead of being the overthrow of human genius by the vagaries of Fortune, the essence of the " moral " provided by the life of Charles XII is simply the defeat of a dreamer by the flaws in his own character.

Nevertheless there is much to admire in the work. From the standpoint of descriptive history it would be hard to beat. Voltaire's eye for the picturesque, and at the same time his infallible perception of the value of details properly selected, are remarkable ; so also is his ability to draw a picture that impresses the imagination by its unity and coherence. There is nothing superfluous, no straining after

[1] Geffroy : *Revue des Deux Mondes* (Vol. LXXXIV).
[2] *Esprit des Lois*, liv. X., Chap. XIV.

effects, no ornamentation, no undue intrusion of the author's opinions, no congestion, no digression : brevity, precision, lucidity, characterize every line. And the result is that the person of Charles XII stands out from the text as if he had been etched on steel. So striking is the portraiture, in its compactness, that M. Geffroy, after reading the more elaborate works produced by Swedish scholars in the nineteenth century, solemnly affirmed his belief [1] that it will never be effaced.

Undoubtedly the magic of style contributed to the success of *Charles XII*—so also did the singularity of the events described ; but it is not because of these things that the book has lived and established its claim to be regarded as an historical work of importance. Its title to fame rests, it may safely be said, on the fact that it is a reliable record. " I can assure you," wrote Voltaire, " that if ever a history merited the trust of the reader, this one does." Subsequent investigations of historians, like Geffroy, have only served to bear out the statement. [2] There was no amount of trouble the author was not prepared to take, in order to ascertain the truth about the transactions that fell under his notice. In addition to the mass of State Paper he consulted— despatches, orders, conventions, and treaties—he made a point of seeking out men who could give him " local colour " and the priceless details which no document could possibly supply. " In history," he remarked, " nothing is to be neglected, and it is necessary to consult, if possible, kings and *valets de chambre*." [3]

[1] *Revue de Deux Mondes* LXXXIV, p. 362 : " Nous avons lu tous ces livres avec l'attention qu'ils méritent, et cette lecture faite, nous ne pensons pas qu'un seul de ces écrivains si estimables pense avoir substitué au livre de Voltaire pour les générations présentes et futures un livre où elles aillent désormais chercher la vivante physionomie du héros suédois."

[2] *Ibid.*, pp. 364-5.

[3] Preface.

Bengesco (*Voltaire—Bibliographie de ses Œuvres*, I., pp. 373-5) gives the following list of authorities consulted :

Original : Memoirs of Fabrice, Poniatowski ; Letters of Fierville, Ville-longue.

Secondary : Adlerfeld, *L'histoire militaire de Charles XII.*
Nordberg, *L'histoire de Charles XII.*
Limiers, *L'histoire de Suède sous la règne de Charles XII.*
Cantemir, *Annales Turques.*

Oral : Baron de Gôrtz, Comte des Alleurs, Maréchal de Saxe, Bolingbroke, Duchess of Marlborough, Dr. Fonseca, M. Bru (first dragoman at the Porte).

From the point of view of Voltaire's future historical writings *Charles XII* must be regarded as essentially a transition work. It marks a definite breach with the old dispensation ; but there is nothing in it of the topic which later became the chief mark of Voltairean history, viz. the progress of manners and of the human mind. We should be justified in calling it an essay in political biography.

The *Siècle* is a much more mature and ambitious undertaking, and in many ways superior to *Charles XII*. To begin with, its history is peculiar ; few books have undergone so great changes in plan and composition between the time of inception and the moment of publication. When he announced his intention of writing it Voltaire had in mind a history of the arts " from Descartes to Rousseau," with the necessary political framework confined to the narrow limits of an introduction. " *L'histoire des arts*," he said, " *voilà mon seul objet*." In this form the book was actually finished in 1738. But in the meanwhile the idea of writing a universal history, suggested to him by the Marquise du Châtelet, began to agitate his mind, and he proceeded to remodel the plan of the *Siècle* with a view to fitting it into the larger scheme. This latter work, which ultimately took shape as the *Essai sur les Mœurs*, was to begin with Charlemagne, where Bossuet had stopped, and to reach its culmination in the reign of Louis XIV, with connecting links still further joining it to contemporary history. The necessary modifications of the *Siècle* resulted in a curtailment of the part dealing with the arts and a corresponding expansion of the political sections. And this is the form in which it was finally published in 1751.

There can be little doubt, however, that the original purpose of the book was not lost sight of. In spite of the fact that thirty out of the thirty-nine chapters of which it consists are devoted to the wars of the reign, the Court, the governmental system, ecclesiastical affairs, and only four to the arts and sciences, it is quite clear that Voltaire did not regard himself merely as the historiographer of Louis XIV. " My object," he writes in the opening sentences of the Introduction, " is to depict to posterity, not the actions of one man, but *the mind of men* [*l'esprit des hommes*] in the most enlightened of centuries." Or, more explicitly still, " I do not consider Louis XIV only as a benefactor of the French, but as a benefactor of mankind : it is as a man I write, not as a subject : *I wish to portray the last century*, and not simply a prince." [1] Thus, the *Siècle* is to be regarded, primarily, as a study of the Age, an apotheosis of the French genius, a gigantic patriotic effusion, with the foreign policy of the reign, the figure of the king, and the affairs of France as the background or starting-point. Its soul lies in the chapters dealing with the arts and sciences, and in particular in the excursion into the culture of Europe, which forms a kind of climax to the whole. If this is the true angle from which to approach it, there never was a more grandiose conception : it is colossal, awe-inspiring, overpowering, and if it had been carried out with anything like the completeness due to it, the *Siècle* would have been one of the great books of the world. Unfortunately it cannot be so regarded ; in spite of the brilliance of the conception and the penetration displayed in the execution it remains a torso. Readers will always find, when they peruse it, that the pleasure to be derived from its pages is mixed with considerable disappointment.

In the first place, it is dangerous to separate off epochs, however important they may appear to be, from the general trend of human affairs ; it has the effect of destroying the unity and continuity of history, and tends to create a totally false impression of the real significance of the transactions described. In history, as in more material things, the principle holds good—*Natura non facit saltum*. Anxiety to exalt the greatness of the seventeenth century constrained Voltaire to make a foil of the preceding age ; with the result that what ought to have been a picture of progressive development becomes a study in contrasts. The intellectual preparation which *culminated* in the wonders of Louis XIV's reign is overlooked, points of contact with the past are lost, the relativity of all historical phenomena is ignored, and events are wrenched from their natural setting, in order to be contemplated independently. In other words, the picture is not historical but ideal ; it represents the vision of a mind which

[1] Voltaire à d'Argenson, 8 Jan., 1740.

dwells habitually on the summits, and fixes its attention on moral and intellectual values rather than on the causal connexions of things. The modern historian rebels against the perpetual insistence upon the "newness," "singularity," and "uniqueness" of the matters related, and clamours for information as to the place of the seventeenth century in the general development of European civilization. Of this there is no indication in the *Siècle*. Voltaire knows, or professes to know, nothing of the long ascent from the twelfth century which brought French culture to the peak where the men of the seventeenth century caught their vision. Hence, while admiring the genius that could grasp so splendid a theme, and the undoubted skill of the execution, critics have been compelled to animadvert upon the false idea underlying the entire work. When all is said and done, the art of painting did not spring "fully armed" from the brain of Poussin, nor sculpture from the chisel of Girardin, nor architecture from the pencil of La Brosse ; and Locke cannot legitimately be called the father of modern philosophy. The fact would appear to be that Voltaire was not equipped to deal competently with the subject he selected ; his knowledge, for all its great sweep and range, was patchy, and in parts strangely defective.

Curiously enough, the weakest section of the *Siècle* is that which deals with the fine arts in Europe. Here it was Voltaire's intention to portray the influence of France on the rest of Europe : to explain, in fact, what he meant by the assertion that the French were, in these matters, the "legislators of Europe." The only way in which this could be done effectively was to examine the *rapports* of French writers and artists with those in surrounding countries, to measure the action and reaction, to conduct, as it were, a physiological investigation into the structure of European culture. But readers of the *Siècle* will look in vain for a systematic appreciation of these *rapports* : they are hardly referred to.

Criticism, however, must be carried still further. Not only is the treatment defective from the formal point of view : the judgments expressed are sometimes so full of personal bias as to be virtually grotesque. One is surprised to learn, for instance, that Addison's *Cato* is " the only English tragedy written with elegance and nobility," that Locke is a greater philosopher than Plato, that Bossuet is to be ranked beneath Bourdaloue as a preacher, or that Swift is Rabelais *perfectionné*. Perhaps the most glaring instance of personal preference is the verdict on Locke. " Locke alone," he writes, " has developed the human understanding in a work in which there are only truths ; and *what renders this work perfect, all these truths are perspicuous*." The implication is obvious : the test of sound philosophy is its Voltairean perspicuity ! [1]

Then, again, there was probably a didactic motive at work which coloured the entire outlook of the writer.[2] French critics have pointed out that in exalting the France of Louis XIV, Voltaire was deliberately passing judgment on the France of his own day. Look on this picture, he seems to say, and on this ! Louis XIV was a Mæcenas of learning, the friend of men of letters, and a generous patron of the arts and sciences ; his degenerate successor, Louis XV, drives men of genius into exile " like Ovid," or imprisons them in the Bastille. " What a world we live in," he exclaimed : " they would burn La Fontaine to-day ! " In other words, Voltaire describes the Age of Louis XIV as a belated Elizabethan, doomed to live under the ascetic *régime* of the Puritans, might have alluded to the halcyon times of Queen Elizabeth—that is, he peopled it with his own ideas, tastes, and desires, frustrated by the ineptitude or tyranny of the government under which he lived. In this view of it the *Siècle* is probably more valuable for understanding the intellectual standpoint of the " Age of Reason " than for the history it contains of the seventeenth century.

Finally, the plan on which the book is written is peculiar, and indicates a striking departure from all previous historical writing, including the *Charles XII*. The first thing that impresses itself on the reader is the abandonment of the principle of continuous narrative. Instead of carrying all events abreast, as his predecessors had done, Voltaire introduces a topical treatment, taking the reader forward along

[1] Chap. XXXIV.　　　　　　　　　　[2] Lanson, p. 115.

successive specified lines, from the beginning to the end of the period. Thus Chapters II–XXIV are devoted to the political and military aspect of the reign ; Chapters XXV–XXVIII describe the private life of the king and the Court ; Chapters XXIX–XXX analyse the governmental system ; Chapters XXXI–XXXIV are concerned with the arts and sciences ; and Chapters XXXIV–XXXIX deal with the Church. The advantage of this *morcellement* is that it brings all the facts together in their logical connexion, and so gives a glimpse, as the subject revolves, of each aspect of the period in its entirety. On the other hand, there are disadvantages more or less inseparable from such a method. The history of a reign, period, or epoch cannot be sawn into lengths with impunity, nor can it be legitimately presented in this way. The unity of the whole is bound to suffer ; and mechanical devices, such as cross references, are necessary if the reader is to be kept aware of the interaction between events and movements classified under different categories. Voltaire was fully conscious of this defect, for occasionally we met with interruptions like *nous verrons dans les chapitres reservées à la vie privée et aux anecdotes comment mourut Louis XIV,*[1] which are distracting. The historian must do more than analyse : he must also integrate—otherwise his work, like the lowest forms of animal organism, will function only by segments. Because of this defect, then, the *Siècle* does not solve the problem of how history should be written. Structurally it is an experiment, a step in advance of the old formless chronological productions of the past, and a move nearer to the unified narrative, interspersed with analysis, which reached so high a perfection in the hands of Gibbon and must remain the ideal of modern historical writing.

It is easy to be hypercritical ; in spite of all that has been alleged against it, the *Siècle* is a great historical work, a noble monument to love of truth and love of country ; and he is a poor critic who allows his mind to dwell on its flaws to the exclusion of its undoubted excellences. As a narrative of

[1] Chap. XXIV; also, " On parlera de ces fanatiques dans le chapitre de la religion " (Chap. XVIII).

events in the reign of Louis XIV it is written with praise-
worthy detachment and sobriety ; seldom does the aggressive
philosophy of the author obtrude itself between the reader and
the facts ; and, above all, one cannot but admire the careful
selection which saves the text from congestion. As Voltaire
himself said, " The chief personages are in the forefront of
the canvas, the crowd is in the background." [1]

Voltaire's preparations for the task he set himself were
enormous. " I have laboured," he wrote in 1751, " like a
Benedictine." He read not only everything published on the
subject—some two hundred volumes in all—but plunged into
the memoirs of Torcy, Villars, Dangeau, Maintenon, the Abbé
de St. Pierre, Berwick, Feuquières, Luxembourg, and others ;
mastered the original papers of Colbert, Louvois, and
Desmarets ; and explored the hitherto untouched documents
of the Louvre relative to the Spanish Succession.[2] Needless
to say, he was also in touch with individuals like Fleury, who
had lived through part of the period described.[3] But the
actual reading of documents and interviewing of witnesses
was only part of the burden. Voltaire found himself confronted with the enormous difficulty of dealing with conflicting and contradictory evidence, which is always at a
maximum when it is a question of recent or contemporary
history. He had also to consider the difficult and delicate
matter of satisfying relatives of the deceased actors, who
imagined that the criticism meted out in the *Siècle* was unjust,
imperfect, or mistaken, or who clamoured for more prominence. " Thirty different correspondences," writes Voltaire, " have I been obliged to carry on after my first edition
was published, all owing to the difficulty of satisfying the
distant cousins of those whose history I had been relating."
To one remonstrant he replied as follows : " Certainly I
shall not make a great man of Valencourt ; he was excessively
mediocre ; *but I shall touch up the part dealing with him to
please you !* "[4]

[1] Voltaire à l'abbé Dubos, 30 Oct., 1738.
[2] *Siècle*, passim.
[3] E.g. " Voici ce que m'a repété plusieurs fois le Marquis de Canillac "
(XXVII) ; or, " Milord Orkney m'a dit que ce corps de troupes," etc. (XIX).
[4] Brougham : *Men of Letters of the Time of George III*, p. 107.

The *Essai sur les Mœurs* [1] is one of the strangest books
ever written by an historian ; and the greatest diversity of
opinion has always prevailed as to its purpose and meaning.
At one time or another it has been described as a *pasquinade*,
a prolonged outrage on the Christian religion, a pamphlet,
a satire on humanity after the manner of *Gulliver's Travels* or
the *Lettres Persanes*, a *jeu d'esprit*, a glorification, in historical
form, of the age in which Voltaire himself lived. [2] In fact,
the only point on which most critics appear to agree is that
it cannot be dignified by the name of a serious history. [3]
Yet when the book is read with care, and not cursorily, it is
difficult to avoid the conclusion that it marks the summit of
Voltaire's achievement as an historian, and his most important
and permanent contribution to the development of history,
both as a science and as an art. From a purely political
biography, cast in a romantic mould, he had passed to the
analysis of an epoch, and from this, again, to a pathological
study of humanity as a whole—a record, it will be admitted,
of expanding horizons, deepening insight, and widening
grasp. At the same time, the reader who embarks on the
Essai soon becomes aware that he has entered upon a radically
different type of history from that of the *Siècle* and the
Charles XII. In the *Essai*, Voltaire is a moralist as well as
an historian ; he assumes the right, not only to describe events,
but also to comment upon, discuss, and criticize them in the
light of contemporary civilization. In short, the *Essai* is a
philosophy of history, rather than a history in the proper sense
of the term. This feature of the book has often proved
repellant to historians, who demand documentary evidence
for every statement, and decry the value of opinion when it is
divorced from the facts. But it would be wrong to assume

[1] Written in sections and published fragmentarily between 1745 and 1756,
under the following titles : *Nouveau Plan d'une histoire de l'esprit humain* ;
Histoire des Croisades ; *Abrégé de l'histoire universelle* ; *Essai sur l'histoire
générale* ; *La philosophie de l'histoire*. The definitive text was issued in 1756
under the title *Essai sur l'histoire générale et sur les mœurs et l'esprit des nations
depuis Charlemagne jusqu'à nos jours*. The edition of 1756 comprised the
Siècle de Louis XIV, and to this was added, in 1763, the *Précis du Siècle de
Louis XV*.—Bengesco, I, pp. 327 *sqq*.
[2] Mably, Chateaubriand, Lanson, etc.
[3] " Der Essai iste voll Bouffonerien und Gaminerien, die einem Feuilleton
besser austehen würden, als einem wissenschaftlichen Werke."—Fueter,
p. 361.

that the character of the *Essai*, as history, was fundamentally affected by its obviously didactic object. Its greatness lies in the fact that it is both a philosophy and a history. The careful and meticulous Robertson, who traversed much the same ground in his Preface to *Charles V*, was impressed by its accuracy and reliability. " I have often followed him as my guide in these researches," he writes ; [1] "and he has not only pointed out the facts with respect to which it was of importance to inquire, but the conclusion which it was proper to draw from them. If he had, at the same time, mentioned the books which relate these particulars, a great part of my labour would have been unnecessary, and many of his readers, who now consider him only as an entertaining and lively writer, would find that he is a learned and *well-informed historian*."

The idea of writing a world history was already well established when Voltaire began his essay. But there was nothing in existence quite like the type of thing he had in mind. The *Annales Mundi* or *Historiæ ab Origine Mundi*, etc., by Chevreau, Puffendorf, and others, were mere chronologies ; and albeit they referred to non-European countries, the references were perfunctory and conventional, due to the desire for geographical rather than historical completeness. [2] If there is to be any comparison between the *Essai* and what preceded it, the only work worth considering is Bossuet's *Histoire Universelle*, written almost exactly one hundred years previously. But what a world of difference there is between the conceptions of the two historians ! The essence of Bossuet's book is its apologetic, its insistence upon supernatural causation, its emphasis of the importance of Jewish, Greek, and Roman history, to the practical exclusion of the ancient East, and its acceptance of Biblical chronology. Voltaire had little difficulty in pointing out the defects of such a constricted view of human affairs. " The illustrious Bossuet," he comments, [3] " who, in his discourse on a part of universal history, seized the true spirit of it, at least in the remarks he makes on the Roman empire, brings his narrative

[1] *History of Charles V.*, Vol. I (end).   [2] Lanson : *Voltaire*, p. 125.
Essai, Avant-propos.

to a close with Charlemagne. But it is necessary to go back
to a more remote period. This eloquent writer, speaking of
the Arabs, who founded so powerful an empire and so flourish-
ing a religion, alludes to them as to a deluge of barbarians.
He appears to have written solely with the intention of
insinuating that everything has been done in the world for
the Jewish nation ; that if God gave the empire of Asia to
the Babylonians, it was to punish the Jews ; if God set up
Cyrus on the throne, it was to avenge them ; if God sent
the Romans, it was, again, to chastise them. That may be
so ; but the splendours of Cyrus and of the Romans have still
other causes," etc. Summarily expressed, Bossuet's history,
for all its impressive eloquence, was only *prétendue universelle*,
its standpoint is unhistorical, and its conception of causation
is false. Voltaire's *Essai* takes us into a totally different
world of thought and imagery. Here we find a complete
reversal of Bossuet's historical assumptions. Taking his
stand on the principle of natural causation, Voltaire throws
overboard all providential interpretations of events, abandons
the Europo-centric point of view, and sweeps into his survey
the history of Chaldæa China and India—countries only
beginning to emerge, as historical entities, from the mists of
antiquity. The result was that he presented the world with
its first systematic attempt to map out the course of human
history on a scientific basis.

The guiding idea of the *Essai*—although it is not easy to
speak of a single idea in this connexion—may be described
as a belief in the law of progress. Throughout its entire
length there runs a more or less explicit comparison between
the *misère du passé* and the *bonheur du présent* ; and the
moral of the story is that the victory of man over the fanaticism, brutality, and crime which soiled the record of the race
for a thousand years is due to the spread of science and the
subordination of all to the dictates of right reason.[1]

There is no doubt that the picture of the past is a dark one ;
but it is by no means so dark as might at first sight appear.
Nor would it be true to say that the *Essai* is essentially an
insult to Christianity. In spite of all his bitter recrimination

[1] Hémon, *Voltaire (Cours de Littérature)*, pp. 41-2.

and sarcastic insinuation against organized religion, Voltaire's references to popes, priests, and monks are not without a recognition, sometimes generous, in most cases just, of their beneficent influence on society.   It is not without a certain shock of surprise, for example, that we come upon his glowing panegyric of Pope Alexander III[1] as the person to whom mankind owes the enjoyment of its rights ; or of Julius II [2] as a "prince of courage and extensive vision."   The promotion of cardinals to the chief office in States elicits not a cutting remark about the worldliness of the Church, but the wise comment, "Churchmen were often better informed and better adapted for affairs than generals and courtiers."[3] Cardinal Sadoleto, again, is styled "a true philosopher, since he was human ; "[4] and bishop Gozlin, a prelate "who fought and died for his country."[5] Even the monastic orders, for which Voltaire cannot be said to have any particular love, are given their place as civilizing agencies during the "Dark Ages." "In these barbaric times," he writes,[6] "when the peoples were so wretched, it was a great consolation to find a secure retreat in the cloisters against tyranny." More emphatically still : "It cannot be denied that there were great virtues in the cloister : there was hardly a monastery which did not contain admirable beings who do honour to human nature. Too many writers have made it a pleasure to search out the disorders and vices with which these refuges of piety were sometimes stained. It is certain that life in the world has always been more vicious, and that great crimes have not been committed in monasteries,"[7] etc. Clearly it would be grossly unfair to say that the *Essai* is simply an attack on religion. The informing spirit which lies behind is that of liberty, toleration, and love of the human race ; justice to all humanitarianism, sympathy with suffering in every shape and form, and a consuming hatred of oppression.

It is patent, however, that the book has its defects, and the defects are serious. To begin with, like the *Siècle*, it lacks

[1] Chap. CXCVII.
[2] Chap. CXIII.
[3] Chap. CXXI.
[4] Chap. CXXXVIII.
[5] Chap. XXV.
[6] Chap. XX.
[7] Chap. CXXXIX.

unity and coherence. The part dealing with ancient history, to which Voltaire gave the title of " Philosophy of History," and set down by way of introduction, has no bearing on the theme developed in the body of the work ; it consists of a series of critical disquisitions on Chaldæa, China, India, Greece, and Rome, without any attempt to link them into a connected account. With Charlemagne we enter at last on the main stream, but only to be disappointed with its aimlessness and want of continuity. Some topics of importance are entirely omitted ; others, again, such as the growth of the Church and its influence on European culture, are handled with scant courtesy and considerable partiality ; while others, like monasticism and scholasticism, are mentioned only incidentally. Moreover, the treatment makes it a not very attractive book to read. " I experienced in reading it," comments the critical Mably,[1] " the boredom of a traveller who, passing from town to town, from province to province, now to the right, now to the left, marches always without knowing where he is going." Possibly the criticism is a trifle malicious ; but the fact that practically the same impression was created in the late Lord Morley's mind is a proof that all is not well with the plan of the *Essai*. " We see," writes the latter,[2] " the towering car drawn slowly along a devious road by the sweat and strain of millions, but we know not why it went by this road rather than another." The fact is, it is difficult to discover any consistent plan in it at all. Sometimes the narrative is purely political, sometimes it divagates into a disquisition on religion, sometimes there is an inquiry into manners and customs, laws, institutions, and the *esprit des peuples* ; but when we try to recollect the drift of the whole our impression is blurred, and we are lost in details, aphorisms, and detached philosophical observations.

[1] *Manière d'écrire l'histoire*, p. 390 (*Œuvres Complètes*, XII).
[2] *Voltaire*, p. 236.

HUME

IT is always difficult to determine how far a school of thought is original and how far derivative. Continental writers are in the habit of claiming that the new historiography was the work of Voltaire, and that all others who participated in the movement were necessarily his disciples. Thus Hume, Gibbon, and Robertson are generally grouped together as the "school of Voltaire in England," while Schlözer, Schmidt, Spittler, and Planck are similarly styled his German followers.[1] We do well to remember, however, that all such classifications are, in the nature of things, more formal than real. They may even be misleading. Undoubtedly, Voltaire was the greatest of the pathfinders. He "blazed the trail," mapped out the country, and opened up the most fertile branches of subsequent investigation. Here, as in so many other matters affecting the intellectual life of his times, he was the most outstanding luminary in the planetary sky of the eighteenth century. But to assert that the British triumvirate were merely his satellites would be grossly unjust. Hume, Gibbon, and Robertson had their own place in the heaven of historical learning, and the light they shed cannot be called borrowed or reflected.

What, for instance, did Hume owe to Voltaire? The evidence of dates shows that the honour of being first in the field belongs to the Frenchman. The *Siècle* had been in the hands of the reading public for the better part of three years before the first volume of the *History of England* made its appearance. The respective dates are 1751 and 1754. Furthermore, it is well known that the *Essai sur les Mœurs* was circulated fragmentarily between 1745 and 1755, although its final and complete issue was delayed until 1756. Presumably, therefore, Hume may have been familiar with the

[1] Fueter, pp. 363 and 371.

contents of both works before he began to write his History.[1]
But is it possible to argue from this external and purely
presumptive evidence to real indebtedness ? By itself
priority in publication proves nothing.

When we turn to the internal evidence, many striking
similarities between the two historians at once present themselves. Both held the same pragmatic and didactic view of
history, and showed the same contempt for mere erudition.
Both, again, entered the domain of history armed with certain
philosophical ideas which they allowed to exercise a controlling and directing influence over their studies. Both expressed
the same bitter hostility to superstition, fanaticism, intolerance ; both condemned all metaphysical, idealistic and
providential interpretations of the human record ; and both
held that positive religion in every shape and form, being an
aberration from the universal and primitive cult of pure
theism, was detrimental to the progress of society. Finally,
both laid supreme stress on " moral factors," and identified
progress with cultural progress.

So striking a correspondence between two writers engaged
in the same field of research, in which one had the advantage
of priority, would seem to indicate either that copying had
taken place on a grand scale, or that both were working
independently on a common stock of ideas belonging to the
age. There is no ground for any intermediate assumption,
such as, for example, that the one borrowed from the other ;
for, in that case, the resemblances would be specific rather
than general. In point of fact, the character of Hume's
thinking effectually disposes of the theory that he either
copied or borrowed ; he was too independent a thinker to
fall under the influence of anyone, however brilliant.[2] Long
before he deserted philosophy for history he had attained
his full stature as an original thinker, and there remained
to be written only the discourse on the Natural History of
Religion, together with a few fugitive essays on " taste,"

---

[1] But note that in the *Essai sur les Mœurs* Voltaire contrasts Hume's
sagacity with the credulity of the monkish historians : " Les moines Fréde-
gaire et Aimon le disent ; mais ces moines, sont-ils des De Thou et des Humes?"
[2] Fueter, p. 365 : " Als sehr warhrscheinlich dürfen wir nur annehmen
dass er die Initiative zu seinem Werke Voltaire verdankt."

" tragedy," and " the passions," in order that his philosophical system might be rounded off. The importance of
this circumstance becomes apparent when it is remembered
that Hume, in common with Voltaire, followed the practice
of writing history *en philosophe*. Even more than in the case
of Voltaire his outlook and method as a historian were pre-
determined for him by his speculative ideas. His philosophy
stands to his history in the relation of a *Prologomenon*, and both,
taken together, represent an organic unity. Instead, therefore, of searching for traces of borrowing from Voltaire
it would be more profitable and practicable to investigate
the extent to which Hume the philosopher guided the pen
of Hume the historian. And this, incidentally, is the method
we shall pursue.

But the independence of Hume may be illustrated from
a different angle. There is abundant testimony to the fact
that his interest in history was native to his genius. From
the first he dabbled in the ancient historians : not systematically, it is true, but purposefully, and with a view to supple-
menting his major studies in philosophy and politics. His
Essays are full of the fruits of such reading.[1] Moreover,
the whole drift of his philosophy was to emphasize the
importance of *data* gained in this way. The raw material
on which his mind worked was drawn partly from observation of life and partly from the great repository and storehouse of fact—history. " Experience, and experience alone,"
says Sir Leslie Stephen,[2] " decided for him questions of
morality and politics." Undoubtedly this predilection for
the concrete and the verifiable was a strong stimulus driving
Hume more and more into a thoroughgoing study of history.
And when at length, disappointed with the indifference of
the public to his philosophical writings, he turned his back on
speculation, the transition to historical research was easy.
It is significant that in 1748, the year in which he made his
last bow as a metaphysician, he penned the following words

---

[1] *Vide* the following : *Of the Populousness of Ancient Nations, that Politics
may be Reduced to a Science, Of the Rise and Progress of the Arts and Sciences,
Of the Balance of Power ;* also his Memorandum Book.
[2] *English Thought,* I, p. 57.

to his friend, Oswald of Dunnikier : [1] " I have *long* had an intention in my riper years of composing some history."

Considerations of a more general character seem to emphasize Hume's independence as a historian. There is a whole heaven of difference between the circumstances under which the two men carried on their historical labours. Voltaire, as we have seen, turned to history because it supplied him with a trenchant and effective weapon in the battle against intolerance, obscurantism, and hypocrisy. History was to him at once a bludgeon for the destruction of unreason and a " platform " from which he might preach the doctrines of the *Enlightenment*, besides being a record of what happened in the past. But to Hume the appeal of Clio was austere and scholarly. In contrast with the violence and vehemence of the French *savant*, he was temperamentally cold, aloof, sceptical ; indifferent to the outward and practical consequences of his views, and absorbed in the satisfaction of his life-long thirst for literary fame. To be instructive and amusing seems to have been his conception of the historian's function. Hume, in fact, was a man of the study, removed for the greater part of his career from the palpitating world of politics in which Voltaire moved like a stormy petrel : or viewing it, as it were, through a glass—darkly and fitfully.

It is not difficult to see that this temperamental difference has a close affinity with basic differences in the intellectual environments of England and France. Great Britain in the latter part of the eighteenth century was a vastly different country from the France of the Bourbons. Under a superficially calm exterior France was seething with suppressed revolution : all her outstanding thinkers were in some sort or other tinged with rebellion against the established order. Chaos reigned in the intellectual world. Optimistic theories of human perfectibility and progress, equally cogent theories of retrogression, gloomy systems of materialism, denunciations of civilization, and sentimental adulations of the " noble savage "—all this confusing medley of thought shows France to have been in the later eighteenth century a veritable hot-bed of discomfort, irritability, and unrest. England, on the

[1] Burton : *Life and Correspondence of David Hume*, Vol. I, p. 236.

other hand, seemed by contrast a land of comparative tranquillity. Factions there were ; but the established order was accepted by all ; the deistic controversy had subsided with the rout of the deists ; Whig and Tory had settled their major differences and agreed to bury the hatchet in a common loyalty to the Hanoverian dynasty. Consequently, while the French writers of the period raised fundamental questions affecting the constitution of society, and thundered against tradition as an evil thing, English writers, contented with the existing framework of society, pursued their speculations unaffected by the distraction of times out of joint.[1]

There is this also to be considered, as affecting the environment in which Hume worked, that the status accorded to literature in England and France differed greatly.   In England politics were the prime interest of all who hoped for social distinction ; literature was slowly rising from the inferior position accorded to a despised profession, and literary men eked out an indifferent livelihood on the crumbs that fell from the hand of a niggardly patronage.[2]   In France the avenues to distinction, the highest prizes society disposed of, were open to wit and talent. Prevented by the prevailing absolutism in the State from participation in political life, the educated classes immersed themselves in art and letters and the feverish cult of new ideas. A thought circulated in a *salon*, and launched upon the world with the combined momentum of the genius who ventilated it and the group of intellectuals who backed it, was like a battering-ram propelled by an army. This distinction is of vital importance to an understanding of the vehemence of French thought and the comparative placidity of English during the century. In England ideas were treated with scant respect by a society intent upon the business of life ; in France they moved the world.

[1] Cf. Burton, I, p. 357 ; II, pp. 207 *et seq.*
[2] " If a man have the misfortune in the former place (i.e. England) to attach himself to letters, even if he succeeds, I know not with whom he is to live, nor how he is to pass his time in a suitable company.   The little company there that is worth conversing with are cold and unsociable ; or are warned only by faction and cabal ; so that a man who plays no part in public affairs becomes altogether insignificant ; and if he is not rich, he becomes even contemptible."—Hume to Blair (Burton, II, p. 268).

THE HISTORY OF ENGLAND

Arguments have been adduced to show that the best way
to teach history is to work from the known to the unknown,
from the institutions, laws and customs with which we are
familiar to their origin in the more or less remote past. It
is not a method that commends itself generally, for, as
Gibbon once said,[1] " In every operation of the mind, there is a
much higher delight in descending from the cause to the effect
than in ascending from the effect to the cause." Nevertheless it was practised by Hume ; he wrote his History, remarked
Horne Tooke,[2] " as the witches say their prayers—back-
wards." The adoption of such a plan has given rise to
various surmises ; for example, that it was deliberately
planned in order to secure for his work an " effective and
persuasive unity,"[3] or, more bluntly, to justify his mis-
representation of the Stuart period by perversions of previous
history—on the assumption, apparently, that one lie can be
cancelled by calling in the aid of many. But there is no need
to impute *mala fides* to Hume : his method was the result of
accident rather than design. He made his *début* as a historian
with the Stuarts because, like Voltaire, he was contemptuous
of the educative value of ancient and barbarous history.
The seventeenth century appealed to him as " the most
curious, interesting, and instructive part of our history,"[4]
the richest in lessons for the statesmen and citizen alike, and
the age in which the public liberty of Englishmen was securely
established.

The story of his great undertaking is as follows. It was
begun in 1752, when Hume became librarian to the Advocates'
Library, Edinburgh, and thereby gained access to one of the
best book collections in Britain. At the outset he was
diffident, in the manner of one making an experiment ; but
as the work progressed and his subject grew upon him he
became more and more convinced that he was creating a new

---

[1] *Miscellaneous Works.*
[2] G. B. Hill : *Letters of David Hume*, p. XXIX, note.
[3] *Quarterly Review*, Vol. LXXIII, p. 536.
[4] Hume to Adam Smith, Sept. 24, 1752.—Burton, I, p. 375.

epoch in English historiography. "The more I advance
in my work," he wrote to a friend,[1] " the more I am convinced that the history of England has never yet been
written ; not only for style, which is notorious to all the
world, but also for matter ; such is the ignorance and partiality of all our historians." [2] By 1756 the first stage of his
long journey was successfully completed : two handsome
volumes on English history from 1603 to 1688 announced that
a new light had appeared in the historical firmament. The
reception accorded to the book was not, however, so warm
as the enthusiastic author had expected. Raucous cries
broke out on all sides that he was a Jacobite in disguise.
" I thought I was the only historian," said Hume,[3] " that had
at once neglected present power, interest, and authority,
and the cry of popular prejudice ; and as the subject was
suited to every capacity, I expected proportionate applause.
But miserable was my disappointment. I was assailed by
one cry of reproach, disapprobation, and even detestation ;
English, Scotch and Irish, Whig and Tory, Churchman and
Sectary, freethinker and religionist, patriot and courtier,
united in their rage against the man who had presumed to
shed a generous tear for the fate of Charles I and the Earl of
Stafford." While the petulant mood was upon him Hume
entertained the idea of leaving England and taking up his
abode in some obscure French village, where he could pursue
his studies undisturbed by the stupidities of his fellow-
countrymen. But his natural buoyancy soon returned, and
he was at work again, preparing the second instalment of
his History. In 1759, the History of the Tudors appeared
in two fresh volumes, with the triumphant announcement :
" I care not to boast, but I will venture to say that I have now
effectually stopped the mouths of all those villainous Whigs
who railed at me." [4] He had discovered, or believed he had
discovered, in his study of the sixteenth century, ample
justification for his views on the constitutional crisis of

[1] Hume to Jas. Oswald, June, 1753.—*Ibid.*, p. 380.
[2] Cf. also (letter to Dr. Clephane, 1753), " Style, judgment, impartiality,
care—every thing is wanting to our historians."
[3] *Autobiography*.
[4] Hume to Robertson, 1759.—Burton, II, p. 50.

Charles I's reign. In reality, his analysis of the powers of the Crown in Queen Elizabeth's day, on which his hope turned, has long since been riddled with criticism and abandoned. But Hume's place on the "English Parnassus" was now so secure, and his historical reputation so great, that he was tempted, at the publisher's instigation, to complete his account of the public transactions of the realm with a volume covering the little-explored period from Julius Cæsar to Henry VII. That he acquiesced with a certain reluctance may be gathered from the remark that he undertook his new task chiefly "as a resource against idleness." [1] Hesitancy was more than justified, because it is doubtful if any author ever set out with less competency than did Hume in this, the last of his historical excursions. Needless to say, he found himself committed to "a work of infinite labour and study." [2] But there was no perfunctoriness in the manner he pursued his task—at least no more than on previous occasions. In 1762 the *History of England from Julius Cæsar to Henry VII* took its place side by side with the volumes on the Stuarts and the Tudors, as an important version of our mediaeval history. The entire work had extended over ten years of Hume's life.

HUME'S CONCEPTION OF HISTORY

As a philosophical and speculative historian Hume is, on a first perusal, somewhat disappointing. He has nothing of the wide range, the imaginative brilliance, the spacious generalization, or the vast panoramic conspectus of history that lend a permanent charm to the historical writings of Voltaire. On the contrary, his vision is limited, his knowledge of general history vague, and he never permits himself to stray from the matter in hand into those illuminating discourses in which Voltaire abounds. To the uninitiated reader he appears in the guise of an eminently attractive historian who places facts above theories, and concentrates on the prime duty of telling a plain tale in a plain and edifying way.

---

[1] Hume to Adam Smith, 28 July, 1759.—*Ibid.*, II, p. 60.
[2] Hume to Andrew Millar, 23 Mar., 1760.—*Ibid.*, II., p. 82.

It is only when the *History of England* is read with a critical
eye that the immense amount of thought involved in it
becomes apparent, and the reader realizes that what seemed
to be a simple, straightforward narrative of fact is really a
highly polished and skilfully articulated philosophy of
history. Moreover, the philosophy is so subtly insinuated
into the texture of the work, so artistically blended with it,
that the task of effecting a separation between them is by
no means easy. We might compare it to a surgical operation
conducted on some vital organ to which all the tissues adhere ;
the whole body is lacerated in the process. Nevertheless,
until this separation has been accomplished, the true bearings
of the *History* are impossible to discover ; its virtues and
vices cannot be appreciated.

Hume's conception of history was determined by several
considerations. To begin with, he believed, after the manner
of Voltaire, that the sole justification for history as a subject
of study consists in its value as an instrument of education.
He was a pragmatist. To be " entertaining and instructive,"
" useful and agreeable," were, in his eyes, the basic principles
of the historian's art. He did not, however, limit the instruction to be derived from history to the improvement of the
intellect : it served also an ethical end—the strengthening
of morals. For Hume, it should be noted, acknowledged no
separation between the intellectual and the moral activities
of man. Virtue, to him, was simply a " more enlarged and
cultivated reason," [1] dependent upon the general development of the mind. Thus the study of history presented itself
to him as a complete culture—entertaining to the fancy,
educative to the mind, and stimulative to virtue. [2] From
which, again, it follows that his supreme concern, as a
historian, was to dwell upon " moral " as opposed to
" physical " causes, that is, on those causes which " operate
on the mind as motives or reasons." [3] Like Voltaire, he will
have nothing to do with the materialist interpretation of

[1] *History of England,* I, p. 222.
[2] *Of the Study of History :* " The advantages found in history seem to be
of three kinds, as it amuses the fancy, as it improves the understanding, and
as it strengthens virtue."
[3] *Of National Character :* " The only observation with regard to the
difference of men in different climates, on which we can rest any weight, is

history. Climate, he says, may work upon the grosser organs of the body, but it cannot affect those " finer organs on which the operations of the mind and understanding depend." History, in short, is a record of the conscious intellectual and moral activities of mankind : a study in ideology.

The consequence of this very carefully delimited conception of what constitutes the *data* of history is that Hume's *History of England* is almost entirely a political narrative, lacking background and explanatory principles. Now, it may safely be assumed that no period of history can be made intelligible without the aid of a multiplicity of factors and a material background of some kind. The stage must be prepared for the action, and the various influences which determined that the drama should be transacted in a particular way, at a particular time and place, must be set forth. We should want to know, for example, why the history of England took the form it did, and why it differed from that of France, let us say, or any other European country.[1] And this can only be made clear if the difference due to geographical situation, racial origin, national character, economic development, etc., are duly brought out. Hume did not grasp the elements of the problem, because he was dominated, as indeed were all the eighteenth century *philosophes*, by the belief that human nature was uniformly the same at all times and places. Why trouble to differentiate, why call in the aid of " materialist " interpretations, if there were no differences worth considering ? Why not treat history on a purely intellectual basis ? The penalty Hume paid for this fallacious assumption is, that he never penetrated to the underlying and ultimately determining conditions of historical development. On the

the vulgar one, that people in the northern regions have a greater inclination to strong liquors, and those in the southern to love and women."
" If we run over the globe, or revolve the annals of history, we shall discover everywhere signs of a sympathy or contagion of manners, none of the influence of air or climate."

[1] Hume sees only similarly : " Lord Bacon, accounting for the great advantages obtained by the English in their wars with France, ascribes them chiefly to the superior ease and plenty of the common people among the former ; yet the government of the two kingdoms was at that time *pretty much alike*."—Essay, *Of Commerce*. Cf. also his comparison between the government of England in the reign of Elizabeth and that of Turkey.—*History*, V, p. 459.

contrary, he exhibits, as Sir Leslie Stephen points out,[1] " an incapacity to recognize the great forces by which History is moulded and the continuity which gives to it a real unity." History, in short, was to Hume an undecipherable hieroglyphic.

But to return to the Humian standpoint. If utility be the basis of historical study, then it may be taken for granted that all periods of history are not of equal importance. There are barren tracts and fruitful tracts : periods that cannot conceivably be made to minister any directly useful lesson or amusement, and others again when the rich variety of events yields a harvest of reflection.[2] In a striking passage of his *History*,[3] Hume pictures the interval between Augustus and the Renaissance as a great trough or depression, in which humanity wallowed for more than a thousand years a prey to ignorance, barbarism, and superstition. The lowest point in this trough occurred, he says, in the eleventh century, " about the time of William the Conqueror." Then by a kind of buoyancy, which he cannot explain except in mechanical terms, society began its toilsome climb to a fresh peak and a fresh vision. " The sun of science, beginning to ascend, threw out many gleams of light, which preceded the full morning, when letters were revived in the fifteenth century." From this picturesque and conventional statement it follows that the Middle Ages, conceived as a period when human genius and achievement were at a low pitch, tend to be regarded as of no account in the history of society. And Hume makes no attempt to conceal his " faint praise " for those who seek to probe into its secrets : they are " ingenious men possessed of leisure," or merely " curious " ; and their investigations, though laudable, have no real value.[4] Civilization, he would say, is the end of the historical process, and must therefore be the theme of the historian. With the obscure and meaningless revolutions of barbarous peoples we need not greatly concern ourselves : they are marked by caprice, bloodshed, cruelty, and they disgust us by their uniformity. Better leave them in the silence and oblivion

---

[1] *English Thought*, I, p. 57.
[2] Vol. III, pp. 298-9.
[3] *History*, Chap. I.
[4] *Ibid.*, Chap. I.

that have befallen them. Moreover, it is a well-known fact that we can never know for certain what actually happened in times of illiteracy ; the records are marred by the low state of morality, and blurred by superstition.[1] Only a cultivated society is able to produce reliable witnesses to truth ; and history in the proper sense of the term can only be written in a rational world.

Of course, Hume must not be taken to mean that the history of the ruder ages is entirely worthless. It has a *negative* value, in the sense that we may learn from it to prize the more the civilization of our own day. " If," he writes,[2] " the aspect of some periods seem horrid and deformed we may thence learn to cherish with the greater anxiety that science and civility which have so close a connexion with virtue and humanity, and which, as it is a sovereign remedy against superstition, is also the most effective remedy against vice and disorder of every kind." But, for all practical purposes, Hume's interest in modern history may be said to begin with the Renaissance,[3] and to deepen the further he leaves behind the realm of conjecture and half lights, and the nearer he approaches to conditions with which he is familiar.

Assuming, then, that he is pre-eminently the historian of civilization, we may go on to ask what he understood by the term. Primarily, he would reply, human happiness : not a Valhalla of luxury and idleness, but a balanced existence, in which material comfort supports moral and intellectual refinement—culture, humanity, and virtue. He does not ignore any aspect of progress entirely. The mechanical arts are necessary to the development of industry and commerce ; and these again, by enlarging the faculties, serve the useful end of promoting the liberal arts. Contrawise, the cultivation of the liberal arts reacts with beneficial effect upon economic progress. " The same age which produces great philosophers and politicians, renowned generals and poets," says Hume, " usually abounds with skilful weavers and ship carpenters. We cannot reasonably expect that a piece of woollen cloth will be wrought to perfection in a nation which

[1] *Ibid.* Vol. I, p. 222.   [2] *Ibid.*, Vol. III, p. 297.
[3] *Ibid.*, Vol. III, pp. 296 and 407.

is ignorant of astronomy, or where ethics are neglected."
But there is no doubt that the hall-mark of a civilized society,
the sign by which we know it, is the cultivation of the arts and
sciences. The more these advance the more sociable men
become : the more they abandon solitude and flock to the
cities, develop their taste in conversation, in clothes, and
furniture, and refine upon their pleasures. In a word, they
" put off the brute, and assume the man."

On the top of this structure of private well-being, pre-
supposing and completing it, comes the perfection of public
life : law, order, police, discipline. " These can never be
carried to any degree of perfection," says Hume, " before
human reason has refined itself by exercise, and by an application to the more vulgar arts, at least of commerce and manufacture." Finally, as the quintessential result of the whole
process, men achieve a softening of their temper, a mildness
of manners, a humane and enlightened existence, which may
be regarded as the *summum bonum* of progress. Factions
are then less inveterate, seditions less frequent, revolutions
less tragical, authority less severe ; and even foreign wars
abate their cruelty. Result : the happiness of the human
race.[1]

It is not difficult to read between the lines of this analysis
that Hume's conception of civilization is simply the idealized
picture of the Age of Reason, with its *salons*, its humanitarianism, its hatred of the " brute facts of the unspoiled
universe," and its insistence on the doctrine that virtue is
simply a form of cultivated reason.

HIS METHOD

Hume's pragmatic view of history had an important
influence on his method of writing it. Like Voltaire, he
quite perceptibly subordinated facts to the doctrine he wished
to convey or to imply. The laborious amassment of detail
and its scientific presentation, logically or chronologically,
was to him both tiresome and irrelevant. " History," he

[1] *Of Refinement in the Arts and Sciences.*

once said,[1] " is a collection of facts which are multiplying without end ; and if they are to be made intelligible, they must, in some way, be abridged." Admittedly ; but what is to be the principle of the abridgment ? To this Hume replies that, just as the scientist invents general theorems and propositions, so the historian must endeavour to " retain the more material events and to drop all the minute circumstances, which are only interesting during the time, or to the persons engaged in the transactions." On the face of it, this is a very plausible suggestion ; but it is justifiable only if we admit that history ought to have a utilitarian object in view. From a modern standpoint it has one serious defect : it is not a principle of selection at all. By leaving the determination of what is important or unimportant to the caprice of the individual it opens the door to purely subjective interpretations of history. And what we get, as a result, is not the " material facts," but those which the writer thinks material —a very different thing. Moreover, such a method is a direct discouragement to research. Why trouble to search out fresh facts if all facts are not potentially valuable ? Yet it is only by continuous investigation, and the revaluation of information already possessed, that the trivial can ultimately be separated from the significant. The process is indeed endless so long as there are records to investigate. To speak of accomplishing the final separation in Hume's day was both premature and presumptuous.

If Hume had made an effort to master the whole range of fact accessible in the eighteenth century something might perhaps be said for the method he employed. But the evidence is conclusive that he made no such attempt. His main supports and sources of information were the histories of Carte, Tyrell, Brady, Spelman, Echard, Rapin, and others ; [2] and if, on rare occasions, he dipped into original authorities, he did so uncritically. " Domesday Book " he notes as being at the Exchequer, but he never saw it, nor could he have used it had he seen it. And when the hitherto unpublished Memorials of James II were put into his hands

---

[1] *History*, Vol. II, pp. 193-4.
[2] *Quarterly Review*, Vol. LXXIII, p. 536 *et seq.*

in Paris he merely " ran over " them and " picked out some
curious passages." [1] Altogether Hume could not be called a
careful worker. There is considerable point in the facetious
remark of a friend of his, when asked to describe the way in
which he wrote the *History* : " Why, mon, David read a vast
deal before he set about a piece of his work ; but his usual
seat was on the sofa, and he often wrote with his legs up ;
and it would have been unco' fashious to have moved across
the room when any little doubt occurred." [2]

Hume's pragmatism appears, again, in his studied effort
to be impartial. If history is to be useful to mankind as an
instructor it must be written by one whose mind habitually
dwells in a serene world beyond the corrosions and corruptions
of party strife, temporal interest, or material advantage of
any kind. The historian must attempt to describe men and
their doings as they might appear from a transcendental, or
absolute, point of view ; or, to paraphrase a somewhat
violent metaphor of Voltaire, he must delineate human
infirmities with the cool insight of a doctor diagnosing disease.
All this Hume not only recognized but fully determined to
carry out.[3] Indeed, he prided himself that on the vital
matter of being impartial he had far out-distanced all his
predecessors. " The first quality of an historian," he says,[4]
" is to be impartial " ; and again,[5] " I may be liable to the
reproach of ignorance, but I am certain to escape that of
partiality."

Alas for the vanity of human anticipations ! Seldom has
a writer been so ruthlessly measured by his own words, or so
bitterly attacked for falling short of them. At first, it is
true, the Continent was warm in its appreciation of the man
who rose above party and wrote history *en homme équitable*.
" In truth," wrote the infatuated Comtesse de Boufflers,[6]
" I believed I had before my eyes the work of some celestial
being, free from the passions of humanity, who, for the benefit

---

[1] Hume to Andrew Millar, 18 Mar., 1764.—Burton, II, p. 200.
[2] *Quar. Rev., ut supra.*
[3] " I have the impudence to pretend that I am of no party and have no
bias."—Burton, I, p. 387.
[4] Hume to Wm. Mure of Caldwell.—Burton, I, p. 409.
[5] Hume to Oswald, June, 1753.—*Ibid.*, I, p. 381.
[6] Burton, I, pp. 95-6.

of the human race, had deigned to write the events of these latter times." But the friendly gestures from Voltaire, Rousseau, and others [1] were soon forgotten amidst the bitter recrimination of English critics, which, beginning in Hume's own day, has lasted uninterruptedly until recent times. Many of the attacks were at first mere lampoons of party men, who found their cherished beliefs and idols trodden upon or ridiculed ; and others may have been motived—as Hume himself imagined—by the " rage against the Scots " then prevalent in England, as a result of Lord Bute's unfortunate administration. [2] But there can be little doubt that the author was largely to blame for the more serious and damnatory criticisms advanced against his book. What confidence could be placed in a writer who, when he came to revise his *History* for a subsequent edition, was compelled to admit [3] that " there is no end of correcting," that " all " his corrections were " invariably to the Tory side," [4] and that his volumes on the Stuarts were so " corrupted with Whig rancour " that he " really deserved the name of a party writer, and boasted without any foundation of impartiality "? [5] He has been taken at his own valuation, and critic after critic has blasted him to posterity as a most false knave, who masked a deliberate partisanship under the guise of philosophic indifference. " As a composition considered *without reference to truth or principle,*" comments one detractor,[6] " his Stuart *apology* is unrivalled." Macaulay's indictment, still more explicit and ruthless, is perhaps the most severe criticism ever passed by one historian on another. " Hume," he says,[7] " is an advocate. Without positively asserting much more than he can prove, he gives prominence to all the circumstances which support his case ; he glides lightly over those which are unfavourable to it ; his witnesses are applauded and encouraged ; the statements which seem

---

[1] G. B. Hill : *Letters of David Hume*, pp. 15, 16.
[2] Hume to Andrew Millar, 14 Jan., 1765.—Burton, II, p. 265.
[3] Hume to Gilbert Elliot, 12 Mar., 1763.—*Ibid.*, p. 146 ; *vide* also p. 434.
[4] *Autobiography.*—Burton, II, p. 144.
[5] Burton, II, p. 145.
[6] Lake : *Quarterly Review*, LXXIII, p. 536.
[7] *Edinburgh Review*, XCIV, pp. 359-60 ; cf. also XII, p. 276, for Jeffrey's criticisms, and XXIV, p. 277, for Fox's.

to throw discredit on them are explained away : a clear and connected abstract of their evidence is given. Everything that is offered on the other side is scrutinized with the utmost severity ; every suspicious circumstance is a ground for comment and invective ; what cannot be denied is extenuated or passed by without notice ; concessions are sometimes made—but this insidious conduct only increases the effect of the vast mass of sophistry." Even Burton, who is more considerate, as befits the author of the *Life and Correspondence*, makes no attempt to palliate the apostasy of his hero ; on the contrary, he accepts the case as proven against him, and puts in a plea for mitigation of the sentence. Hume, he contends, fell a victim to the seductive influence of the gentlemanly and scholarly Clarendon, and allowed his sympathies for the misfortunes of the Stuarts to overbear his integrity as a philosopher. " As he went on with his narrative," writes Burton,[1] " he found on one side refinement, an elevated and learned priesthood, a chivalrous aristocracy, a refined court "—all the " divinity " that " doth hedge a king," followed by all the sad solemnity of fallen greatness— an adverse contest, borne with steady courage, and humiliation and death endured with patient magnanimity. On the other side appeared plebeian thoughts, rude, uncivil speech, barbarous and ludicrous fanaticism, and success consummated by ungenerous triumphs. His philosophic indifference gave way before such temptations and he went the way of his sympathies." And so, in order to save Hume from the imputation of deliberate falsity, we are invited to regard him as a mawkish sentimentalist !

Fortunately there is another way out of the difficulty, which makes it unnecessary to invoke either knavery or sentimentalism. Hume's idea of impartiality was peculiar. It did not consist in establishing truth of fact—the sense in which we should use the word to-day—so much as truth to certain philosophical convictions from which he started as first principles. The conclusion is not that he falsified history either intentionally or involuntarily, but that he was bold enough to measure characters and events against a more or

---

[1] *Life and Correspondence*, Vol. I, p. 404.

less absolute standard, and to make such adjustments as he deemed necessary, in order to achieve a greater correspondence between theory and reality. It is not the method a modern historian would, for a moment, think of employing ; but it was the way in which the eighteenth century *philosophe* envisaged his task ; and it suggested that we should suspend judgment until we have examined the bearing of his philosophy on his history.

THE RELATION BETWEEN HUME'S METAPHYSICS AND HIS HISTORY

The core of Hume's metaphysics is, by common consent, to be found in his theory of causation. Starting from the Lockian position that knowledge of the world is built up originally on experimental evidence afforded by the senses, he asserts that the only relationship between objects, traceable beyond the senses, is that of cause and effect[1] ; on this all our reasonings concerning matter of fact or existence are founded.[2] But when we say that one object is the cause of another we do not mean that it produces it ; for in nature there is no *a priori* connexion between things. On the contrary, everything is at first separate, distinct, and without filiation.[3] All we imply, therefore, when we postulate a causal connexion, is that we have observed it to be customary *in our experience* that event A follows event B ; and from this customary succession we infer the dependence of the one on the other.[4] The object *flame*, we remember, is accompanied by the sensation *heat* ; without more ado we connect them together as cause and effect.[5] But the sole connexion between them is succession in time. Hume was careful to point out that his theory did not involve the absurd conclusion that anything may be the cause of anything. On the contrary, it implied a belief in the uniformity of nature. This latter doctrine he lays down as an axiom or first principle. " Our idea of necessity and causation," he remarked,[6] " arises

---

[1] *A Treatise of Human Nature*, p. 74.
[2] *Enquiry Concerning the Human Understanding*, p. 76.
[3] Ibid., p 74.   [5] *Ibid.*, pp. 74 and 75.
[4] *A Treatise*, etc., p. 87.   [6] *Enquiry*, etc., p. 82.

entirely from the uniformity observable in the operations of nature, where similar objects are constantly conjoined together, and the mind is determined by custom to infer the one from the appearance of the other."

There are, of course, apparent exceptions to the uniformity displayed in nature—" irregularities," which seem to indicate the possibility of lapses from law. But Hume will not allow any such assumption. Chance, in the sense of something happening without a cause, is an absurdity. When we use this word we merely mean that " secret causes " [1] are at work, whose operation we cannot fully grasp owing to the infirmity of our minds. Thus the physician is not surprised when he finds himself baffled by symptoms, or when medicines fail to produce the result expected from them. He does not deny the uniformity of the principles by which the animal economy is governed ; he simply concludes that the human machine is mightily complicated, and that the " springs and principles " by which it is operated are often hidden by reason of their minuteness or remoteness. [2] Without, therefore, presuming to understand the ultimate causes of things, which are " totally shut up from human curiosity and enquiry," [3] we may safely act on the assumption that the universe is based upon law and prosecute our search for proximate causes. This, in fact, is what the scientist does ; and the information so gained is of the greatest value in enabling mankind to regulate and control future events.

Now, if this theory of knowledge is to be valid it must apply to the domain of human action as well as to nature. There must be discernible in history a uniformity and regularity of recurring phenomena similar to that observable in the natural world, and this, again, implies two important suppositions : (1) that the mind of man is the scene of a uniform play of motive ; and (2) that the motives of men in the mass are quantitatively and qualitatively the same for all times and all countries. Only if both conditions hold good is it possible to subject the course of history to a rigorous scheme of causation and to build up from it a series of general laws. Hume boldly accepts both conditions, and

[1] *Ibid.*, pp. 56, 58, and 87.   [2] *Ibid.*, p. 87.   [3] *Ibid.*, p. 103.

proceeds to draw the necessary inferences. The following passage will make his position clear. " It is," he says,[1] " universally acknowledged that there is a great uniformity among the actions of men in all nations and ages, and that human nature remains still the same in its principles and operations. *The same motives always produce the same actions : the same events follow from the same causes.* Ambition, avarice, self-love, vanity, friendship, generosity, public spirit : these passions, mixed in various degrees and distributed through society, have been from the beginning of the world, and still are, the causes of all the actions and enterprises which have ever been observed among mankind. Would you know the sentiments, inclinations, and course of life of the Greeks and Romans ? Study well the temper and actions of the French and English : you cannot be mistaken in transferring to the former most of the observations you have made with regard to the latter. . . . *Mankind are so much the same in all times and places that history informs us of nothing new or strange in this particular.* . . . Nor are the earth, water, and the other elements, examined by Aristotle and Hippocrates, more like those which at present lie under our observation than the men described by Polybius and Tacitus are to those who now govern the world."

As a principle of historical investigation this so-called constancy of human nature is of capital importance. On the strength of it Hume lays down the rule that, just as we refuse to believe in the authenticity of any event that contradicts nature, so also we should be right in denying the historical truth of any report that runs counter to accepted standards of human motive and action. If, for example, a traveller from foreign parts tells of the existence of men wholly different from those we are acquainted with—men who act uniformly from motives of friendship, generosity, and public spirit, who shun avarice, ambition, and revenge—we should be entitled to doubt his tale and call him a liar, with as much certainty as if he had stuffed his story with dragons, centaurs, miracles and prodigies.[2] The basis of historical truth, in this particular, is a thoroughgoing know-

[1] *Ibid.*, pp. 83-4.   [2] *Ibid.*, p. 84.

ledge of human nature. The historian must know men
intimately if he is to write about them correctly. He must
be able " to mount up to the knowledge of their inclinations
and motives, from their actions, expressions, and even
gestures," and to " descend " again " to the interpretation of
their actions from a knowledge of their motives and inclinations." Fortified with this information he will be able to
strip transactions of their glamour ; discriminate what is
miraculous from what is merely marvellous ; brush aside
veils and pretexts, and penetrate to the real influences shaping
conduct ; detect deceit and hypocrisy at work beneath a
show of benevolence, self-interest beneath altruism ; and so he
will be able to give to truth and virtue their true weight in
history, but no more than their true weight.[1]

But it is not easy, as Hume admits, to trace cause and effect
in the historical world ; and the historian can never be quite
sure that his conclusions are just. Custom, education, sex,
youth and age, health and sickness, exaltation and depression of spirits—all have their effect on the result. And in
addition to these more or less calculable factors there are
" secret causes " at work, as in the natural world, which
baffle the investigator.[2] " Nothing requires more nicety,"
says Hume,[3] " in our enquiries concerning human affairs,
than to distinguish exactly what is owing to chance and what
proceeds from causes ; nor is there any subject in which an
author is more liable to deceive himself by false subtleties
and refinements." In order to facilitate investigation he
lays down a general rule, which will enable the distinction
to be made with the minimum of error, viz. " What depends
upon few persons is, in a great measure, to be ascribed to
chance, or secret and unknown causes ; what arises from a
great number may often be accounted for by determinate
and known causes."[4]

But the principal consequence of Hume's doctrine of
uniformity as applied to history is this : if, as he asserts,
human nature is a constant quantity, composed of certain
qualities or powers which, in the sum total, are the same for

---

[1] *Ibid.*, pp. 84-5 ; Essay, *Of Public Credit.*   [2] *Enquiry*, pp. 85-6.
[3] Essay, *Of the Rise and Progress of the Arts and Sciences.*   [4] *Ibid.*

all epochs and countries, it follows that history is simply a repeating decimal. The great drama is transacted on a flat and uniform level; each age or group working up into forms that are already familiar the common stock of attributes. That Hume believed this to be so is apparent from his remark that the chief use of history is " only to discover the constant and universal principles of human nature by showing men in all variety of circumstances and situations."[1] Now it is only necessary to consider this latter thesis for a moment in order to realise its speciousness. It does not follow that because the springs of human action are always the same human nature is therefore unchangeable. The flaw in the reasoning arises from a false and mechanical psychology. To Hume, character appears in the light of an assemblage of virtues and vices, in the same way as an object is the sum of its qualities. The modern psychologist would take a very different view. He would insist upon unity as a *sine quâ non*; he would point out that personality always acts as an organized unit, albeit under the influence of one or more dominating motive or motives; and the consequence is that whereas Hume regards the human soul as reproducing the same or similar acts, from one end of the historic epoch to the other, the modern philosopher would assert that it continually brings fresh phenomena to the light : in each case the quality and intensity of the action depending upon the motive or motives that have gained the upper hand.

Hume, therefore, lays himself open to the same criticism as Voltaire. There is no parity between the conduct of a Greek or Roman and that of an Englishman or Frenchman : still less between a modern and a mediaeval man. The quality of their acts is different, even although the qualities with which they are endowed are the same. But Hume could not see this. In virtue of his theory of uniformity he takes his stand on the existence of a normal historical man, as arbitrary and fanciful as the so-called economic man of the old political economy. And the error vitiates his conception of the past, as it vitiated Voltaire's. He will not allow for any irrational element that breaks up the chain

[1] *Enquiry*, p. 84.

of causation ; every character he meets in history must be reduced to type. If strange motives or incomprehensible deeds are encountered, which cannot be squared with the standard his philosophy has evolved, he at once proceeds to explain them away as aberrations, or as dependent upon peculiar circumstances. " When men depart," he says, " from the maxims of human reason, and affect *artificial lives* . . . no one can answer for what will please or displease them. They are in a different element from the rest of mankind : and the natural principles of their mind play not with the same regularity as if left to themselves, free from the illusions of religious superstition or philosophical enthusiasm."[1]

In order to see the method at work, let us take two well-known personages in history whose characters must obviously create a problem for Hume, viz. Luther and Joan of Arc. Neither can be measured with the standard applicable to the mass of human beings. How does Hume reconcile them with his principle of uniformity ? Here is his picture of Luther :[2]

Martin Luther, an Austin friar, professor in the University of Wittenberg, resenting the affront put upon his order, began to preach against the abuses in the sale of indulgences ; and being naturally of a fiery temper, and provoked by opposition, he proceeded even to decry indulgences themselves ; and was thence carried, by the heat of the dispute, to question the authority of the pope, from which his adversaries derived their chief arguments. Still, as he enlarged his reading in order to support these tenets, he discovered some new abuse or error in the church of Rome ; and finding his opinions greedily hearkened to, he promulgated them by writing, discourse, sermon, conference ; and daily increased the number of his disciples. All Saxony, all Germany, all Europe, were in a very little time filled with the voice of this daring innovator ; and men, roused from that lethargy in which they had so long sleeped, began to call in question the most ancient and most received opinions. . . . And Luther, a man naturally inflexible, vehement, opinionative, was become incapable, either from promises of advancement, or terrors of severity, to relinquish a sect, of which he himself was the founder, and which brought him a glory, superior to all

[1] *A Dialogue.* [2] *History*, Vol. IV, pp. 37-9.

others, the glory of dictating the religious faith and principles of multitudes.

It is difficult to detect any actual misstatement in this description ; it is remarkably true and effective so far as it goes. But how great are the omissions ! We are asked to believe that the success of the Reformation depended chiefly on the personality of Luther ; and not so much on his personality after all, as upon the *accidents* of his personality. Not a word, it will be observed, is uttered concerning the great informing convictions which gave the reformer his identity and distinction as a leader of a *religious* movement. Nor is it possible to realize from the description that the action took place in the sixteenth century. In accordance with Hume's philosophical theory the universal is emphasized, the local and particular are suppressed, and all sense of perspective is obliterated. But note especially how ingeniously the picture is drawn, so as to convey the precise impression the artist desires to convey. With masterly skill the reader's attention is diverted from Luther's beliefs and fixed on his temperament ; that is, on the qualities he shared with all men, only in a more pronounced degree. He has a " fiery temper " ; he is " carried by the heat of the dispute " ; " he enlarges his reading in order to support his tenets " ; " he finds his opinions greedily hearkened to " ; he " increases the number of his disciples " ; he fills Saxony, etc., with his " voice " ; he in " inflexible," " vehement," opinionative " ; he is " incapable of abandoning " the sect he leads, " because it brings him the glory of dictating the religious faith and principles of multitudes." In short, there is no mystery about Luther at all : he is simply *l'homme sensuel moyen*, who wins through by dint of egoism.

Or, take the equally famous passages about Joan of Arc.[1] Here again, the analysis is brilliant, the composition of the picture masterly ; but there is no attempt to exhibit the distinctive qualities of Joan's genius—she is reduced to type, or explained away. Nor is it possible to realize from the description that she lived in the fifteenth century : it is too

[1] *History*, Vol. III, pp. 141-7.

generalized   Joan is a peasant girl " accustomed to horses "
at the village inn of Domrémy.   She is moved by the misfortunes of the King (Charles VI), who is " by nature inclined
to friendship and the tender passions," and thereby " the
hero of that sex, whose generous minds know no bounds in
their affections."   Seized by a " wild desire " to help her
sovereign, " her inexperienced mind working day and night
on this favourite object," she " mistakes the impulses of
passion for heavenly inspirations."   She " fancies " she
sees visions ; and possessing an " uncommon intrepidity of
temper," she throws off the " bashfulness and timidity
natural to her sex, years, and low station," etc.   The effect
of her appearance on the English is at first to excite them
to ridicule of the French for entrusting their destiny to a
woman ; but they " felt their imaginations secretly struck
with the vehement persuasions which prevailed around
them," and wait " with an anxious expectation, not unmixed
with horror," for the issue.   The English general, Suffolk,
" instead of banishing these vain terrors by hurry, and
action, and war," waits until his men " recover from panic,"
and thereby allows their prepossessions to sink deeper into
their minds.   Thus the English find their courage " daunted
and overwhelmed," and " infer " that a divine vengeance is
hanging over them.   The French " draw the same inference
from their enemy's inactivity."   Hence " the spirit resulting
from a long course of uninterrupted success was on a sudden
transferred from the victors to the vanquished."

We have noted, in passing, that Hume's psychology was
mechanical and false.   His conception of character as the
sum of certain qualities " mixed in varying proportion " not
only led him into the subtleties just alluded to, it also resulted
in a curiously mechanical method of describing the traits
of the historical personages who enter into his story.   As
a rule, he does little more than enumerate their virtues and
vices, making no attempt to create personalities at all.
Thus, when he has finished a character sketch, what stands
out from the canvas is not a real person, but a dexterously
poised, mechanically sustained assemblage of divergent,
disconnected, or conflicting qualities.   We are compelled to

admire the ingenuity, the logicality, and the literary skill displayed in the delineation ; but the result is nevertheless artificial, unreal, and unconvincing to a degree. Consider, for example, the character of James I as Hume sees it : [1] " Many virtues, it must be owned, he was possessed of ; but scarce any of them pure, or free from the contagion of the neighbouring vices. His generosity bordered on profusion, his learning on pedantry, his wisdom on cunning, his pacific disposition on pusillanimity, his friendship on light fancy and boyish fondness. . . . His capacity was considerable ; but fitter to discourse on general maxims than to conduct intricate business : his intentions were just ; but more adapted to the conduct of private life than to the government of kingdoms. Awkward in person and ungainly in his manners, he was ill qualified to command respect ; partial and undiscerning in his affections, he was little fitted to acquire general love. Of a feeble temper more than of a frail judgment : exposed to our ridicule from his vanity ; but exempt from our hatred by his freedom from pride and arrogance. And upon the whole, it may be pronounced of his character, that all his qualities were sullied by weakness and embellished by humanity." How much nearer are we brought by this epigrammatic and highly-finished picture to the personality of the king ? Every nook and cranny in his nature is explored ; nothing is omitted of importance ; and yet there is no illumination, no central idea or informing principle to create unity and attach the various virtues and vices to each other. James is still an enigma.

Sometimes, it is true, Hume introduces more artistic integration into his character studies ; as, for instance, in his portrayal of Cromwell [2] or the second Duke of Bucking-

---

[1] *History*, Vol. VI, pp. 153-4.

[2] " Carried by his natural temper, to magnanimity, to grandeur, and to an imperious and domineering policy ; he yet knew, when necessary, to employ the most profound dissimulation, the most oblique and refined artifice, the semblance of the greatest moderation and simplicity. A friend to justice, though his public conduct was one continued violation of it ; devoted to religion, though he perpetually used it as an instrument of his ambition ; he was engaged in crimes from the prospect of sovereign power, a temptation which is in general irresistible to human nature. And by using well that authority which he had attained by fraud and violence, he has lessened, if not overpowered, our detestation of his enormities by our admiration of his success and of his genius."—*History*, VII, pp. 29, 30.

ham.[1] But defective psychology prevented him from grasp-
ing any character as a unity ; and the integration he achieves
is more verbal than real.

HUME'S ATTITUDE TO RELIGION AND ITS INFLUENCE ON HIS HISTORY

The best way of describing Hume's religious position is
to say that it was a contemplative joy in the fitness of things—
the manifest orderliness and functional regularity of nature.
Like Voltaire, he believed in the existence of an intelligent
First Cause, who set the Cosmos in motion and placed it
under the dominion of inflexible law. " A purpose, an
intention, a design," he remarks,[2] " is evident in everything :
and when our comprehension is so far enlarged as to contemplate the first rise of this visible system, we must adopt,
with strong conviction, the idea of some intelligent cause or
author." He does not believe that it is possible either to
prove the existence of this *deus ex machinâ*, or to establish
relations with it ; nor will he admit that human affairs are
in any way directly influenced by it. Consequently he
concludes : (1) that miracles, being violations of natural
law, are *ipso facto* incredible,[3] or acceptable only among
barbarous or ignorant peoples ;[4] (2) that religious belief
is entirely a thing of faith, incapable of defence on rational
grounds ;[5] and (3) that those who claim a special illumination
are either deluded by an inflamed imagination or are deliberate
impostors, i.e. either fools or knaves.[6] And so Hume comes,
by much the same path as Voltaire, to the general position,
that all the positive religions of the world are aberrations or
fallings-away from the pure theistic belief, which it is the

---

[1] *Ibid.*, VII, p. 459.
[2] *Natural History of Religion :* Philosophical works (1826), IV, p. 510.
[3] " A miracle is a violation of the laws of nature ; and as a firm and unalterable experience has established these laws, the proof against a miracle, from
the very nature of the fact, is as entire as any argument from experience can
possibly be imagined."—*Of Miracles*, Part I.
[4] *Enquiry*, p. 119.
[5] " Our most holy religion is founded on faith, not on reason ; and it is
a sure method of exposing it to put it to such a test as it is, by no means,
fitted to endure."—*Enquiry*, p. 130.
[6] *Of Miracles*, Part I.

province of the intellect alone to manifest and maintain.
" Examine," he says,[1] " the religious principles which have
in fact prevailed in the world.   You will scarcely be persuaded
that they are anything but sick men's dreams : or perhaps
you will regard them as playsome whimsies of monkeys in
human shape, rather than the serious, positive, dogmatical
asseverations of a being who distinguishes himself with the
name of rational."

Needless to say, this extremely attenuated conception of
religion, together with its concomitant condemnation of all
positive expressions of belief, led to a singularly blatant
inability on Hume's part to understand the working of the
religious mind in history, or to give to Christianity its place
among the forces shaping civilization.   He understood
perfectly the cult of nature-worship among savages ; it
was the outcome of the impact on the untrained mind of
natural convulsions, plagues, and pestilences ; but of the
historical transformation of this raw material of religion into
the elaborate, moralized, and dogmatical religions of the
civilized world he seems to have known and cared little.   In
his estimation, the proper function of religion, as it exists
in the modern world, is to purify the heart and to secure
obedience to the law ; and if it pursues this useful purpose
faithfully it must of necessity remain a silent and secret
influence working, as it were, beneath the surface of society.
The purer it is the less it ought to enter into the annals of war,
politics, intrigues, revolutions, and the other world-shaking
concerns, which furnish the historian with his stock-in-
trade.[2]

Why, asks Hume, should religion create divisions among
men ?   Two persons travelling on the same road, in opposite
directions, pass each other easily if the way be broad enough ;
how is it that two men who happen to hold different religious
views cannot pass without shocking ?   The way, one would
think, is wide enough to accommodate both.[3]   And what
justification is there for the existence of religious parties ?
Political parties are founded upon *interest*, and they stand

[1] *Philosophical Works*, IV, 512.   [2] Burton, II, pp. 11-13.
[3] *Of Parties in General.*

for different policies; but religious parties are founded
upon *principle*, and they do not stand for any difference in
conduct: their difference is entirely speculative.[1] Worse
still, the points over which men dispute in matters of religion
are absurd and unintelligible even to themselves. " Civil
Wars which arose some few years ago in Morocco between
the *Blacks* and *Whites*, merely on account of their complexion," comments Hume,[2] "are founded upon a pleasant
difference. We laugh at them; but, I believe, were things
rightly examined, we afford much more occasion of ridicule
to the Moors. For what are all the Wars of religion, which
have prevailed in this polite and knowing part of the world ?
They are certainly more absurd than the Moorish Civil Wars.
The difference of complexion is a sensible and real difference ;
but *the controversy about an article of the faith, which is utterly
absurd and unintelligible, is not a difference in sentiment, but
in a few phrases and expressions, which one party accepts
without understanding, and the other refuses in the same manner."*

Still more significant, from the standpoint of Hume's
treatment of religion in his *History*, is the distinction he draws
between " superstition " and " enthusiasm "—" two species
of false religion." Both, he tells us,[3] are based on human
ignorance ; but whereas the former battens on fear, weakness,
and melancholy, and by rendering men submissive, favours
the growth of priestly power, the latter, arising from hope,
pride, presumption, and a warm imagination, leads to the
establishment of individual freedom. One point, however,
they have in common—they both cause cruel disturbances in
the body politic ; and on grounds of social utility they are
to be condemned.[4] The importance of the distinction will
be clearer if we consider briefly the account he gives of the
Reformation.[5]

Ordinarily in writings on this subject the Reformation is
discussed from a dogmatic or moral point of view, or from
both standpoints. But Hume has nothing whatever to say

---

[1] *Ibid.*   [2] *Ibid.*   [3] *Of Superstition and Enthusiasm.*
[4] Hume is never so animated as when he is castigating the excesses of
fanaticism—either of the Scottish Covenanters or the Irish Catholics.—
History, Vol. VI, pp. 436-44 ; VII, pp. 178-83 ; VIII, pp. 113-14.
[5] *Ibid.*, Vol. IV, pp. 37-9.

on the justice or efficacy of the Protestant arguments, or on the alleged moral superiority of the reformers. To him the battle was between two false religions : Catholic *superstition*, on the one hand, and Protestant *enthusiasm* on the other. Reason and reflection played no part in it. Consequently the eventual success of the Protestants was due, not to the validity of their case, but to a multitude of circumstances which played into their hands : the existence of the printing press, the fact that men were just awakening from slumber and prepared to accept any novelty, the dawning of the critical spirit, the vehemence of the Protestant denunciations, the assumption of superior piety, the encouragement given to the civil power to fall upon the wealth of the Church, etc. In fact, the continental Reformation had no attraction for Hume : it was devoid of philosophic interest. On the other hand, the English movement appealed to him by its practicality and moderation.[1] " Of all the European Churches which shook off the yoke of papal authority," he writes, " no one proceeded with so much reason and moderation as the Church of England ; an advantage which had been derived partly from the interposition of the Civil magistrate in this innovation, partly from the gradual and slow steps by which the reformation was conducted in that kingdom." He applauds the restraint placed in the " popular rage " by the government, the preservation of the hierarchy, the ancient liturgy, and ceremonies that centuries rendered venerable ; and he dwells on the fact that no innovation was permitted that savoured of spite or mere opposition to former usage. Thus, " the new religion, by mitigating the genius of ancient superstition, and rendering it compatible with the peace and interests of society, had preserved itself in that happy medium which wise men have always sought, and which the people have so seldom been able to maintain."

On the same grounds on which he defends the Settlement of the sixteenth century Hume is led to condemn the Puritans who first challenged, and then overthrew, it. For the sake of " a garb, a gesture—nay, a metaphysical or grammatical distinction "—they plunged the Church and the nation into

[1] *History*, Vol. IV, pp. 149-50.

chaos for more than sixty years.[1] But his case against the Puritans is more radical than might appear. Although he cannot be styled a lover of ceremonial, he was opposed on utilitarian grounds to the extreme simplification of worship clamoured for, and subsequently introduced, by this party. It was dangerous, he believed, to society and detrimental to the individual.[2] Straining after an impossible devotion, seeking rapturous glimpses of divine truth, only to sink back again into gloom, despising all external aids to the mind, so absorbed in the inner life that they fled from society and everything that could soften and humanize the character, the Puritans were, in Hume's eyes, not only proper objects of the philosopher's contempt and sarcasm, but, in a very real sense, "enemies of the human race."[3] On the other hand, "whatever ridicule may be thrown on pious ceremonies, it must be confessed, that during a very religious age, no institutions can be more advantageous to the rude multitude, and tend more to mollify that fierce and gloomy spirit of devotion, to which they are subject."[4] Hence, by following out his criterion of utility, Hume arrives at the unexpected conclusion that Laud and his associates were benefactors of the nation. They provided the " affrighted and astonished mind " with something sensible to hold by when the object of its devotion eluded its grasp. Moreover, the relaxation of the mind in the contemplation of pictures, vestments, postures, and impressive buildings was not merely philosophically justifiable : it gave a stimulus to the fine arts which minister to religion.[5]

It will be clear, then, that Hume's antipathy to religion as a force in human affairs is not of a blind and uncompromis-

---

[1] *Ibid.*, Vol. V, p. 154 ; and VI, p. 389.
[2] *Ibid.*, VI, p. 85.
[3] *Vide* the following satirical, ironical, savage, and abusive passages : Vol. VI., pp. 299, 425-6 ; VII, pp. 5, 9, and 227. Hume's rooted distrust of puritanism is summarily expressed in the following sentences : " Religious ecstasies, if constantly employed, must often be counterfeit, and must be warped by those more familiar motives of interest and ambition, which insensibly gain upon the mind."
" Hypocrisy quite pure and free from fanaticism, is perhaps, except among men fixed in a determined philosophical scepticism, then unknown, as rare as fanaticism entirely purged from all mixture of hypocrisy."
[4] *History*, Vol. VI, p. 41.
[5] *Ibid.*, p. 42.

ing variety. It was only when it became an obstruction to progress, and a breeder of civil turmoil, that he vented his wrath on it. But let the actions of churchmen contribute ever so slightly to the cause of progress, as he conceived it— that is, to public tranquillity, material well-being, culture, and virtue—and his attitude will, in general, be both sympathetic and appreciative. Thus while he condemned all outbursts of popular " frenzy,"[1] while he was always on the alert to unmask the schemer behind the saint, and while he lamented the tribute paid to the memory of " pretended saints " and the comparative lack of enthusiasm for the man of genius and the wise legislator,[2] he was wise enough to see that frequently in the course of history the clergy were the guardians of liberty and the saviours of society. " It must be acknowledged," he writes,[3] " that the influence of the prelates and the clergy was often of great service to the public. Though the religion of that age (i.e. mediaeval times) can merit no better name than that of superstition, it served to unite together a body of men who had great sway over the people, and who kept the community from falling to pieces, by the factions and independent power of the nobles."

HUME'S POLITICAL PHILOSOPHY AND ITS RELATION TO HIS HISTORY

If Hume's ethical theory rests upon the general principle that utility is at once the end and the justification of moral action, his political thinking is saturated with the same doctrine.[4] He repudiated the Whig formula that political obligation is founded upon a contract between ruler and

[1] E.g. the Crusades ; *History*, Vol. I, p. 311.

[2] " It is indeed a mortifying reflection to those who are actuated by the love of fame . . . that the wisest legislator, and the most exalted genius, that ever reformed or enlightened the world, can never expect such tributes of praise, as are lavished on the memory of pretended saints, whose whole conduct was probably, to the last degree, odious and contemptible, and whose industry was entirely directed to the pursuit of objects pernicious to mankind."—*History*, Vol. I, pp. 421-2 : Verdict on Becket.

[3] *History*, Vol. II, p. 157.

[4] Hume's political ideas are to be found particularly in the following writings : *A Treatise of Human Nature*, III, §§ vii-ix ; *Of the Original Contract ; Of Passive Obedience ; Idea of a Perfect Commonwealth ; Of the Protestant Succession ; Of the Coalition of Parties ; Of the Origin of Government.*

ruled, and also the Tory view that grounded it upon a divine sanction. The State, he argued, is simply a creation of man's enlightened self-interest—a contrivance whereby his vision is artificially lengthened beyond the immediate and contiguous. It exists to guarantee stability of possession, freedom to transfer property, and the performance of promises : in a word, justice. " We are, therefore," he remarks, " to look upon the vast apparatus of our government as having ultimately no other object or purpose but the distribution of justice." The contract theory he dismissed as nonsensical and unhistorical. Preach it to-day, he says, in most parts of the world, and you will be regarded as either seditious or delirious : there never has been any such agreement or understanding in history. Men will tell you that they did not contract themselves into obedience : they were born into it. An equally damaging criticism is, of course, brought against the divine right school. Those who plead a special sanctity for the authority of princes, says Hume, or who speak of a " rigid loyalty to particular persons and families," are bigots or superstitious persons. There is no special sacredness attaching to kingly authority : a magistrate, a constable, nay, even a robber or a pirate, exercise their respective functions in virtue of an equally divine commission and indefeasible right. On the other hand, pursue the history of any government back to its origin and you will find it begin in an act of usurpation or conquest ; for, says Hume, force and violence play a dominant part in all political changes.

Having thus stripped the veil from the face of political obligation, what does he supply in its place ? Upon what does the duty of obedience rest ? It rests, he asserts, upon the protection and security we enjoy as citizens—protection and security we could not hope to possess if we were perfectly free and independent units. From which it follows that, although the idea of a contract is false, the continuance of our allegiance as subjects depends upon the maintenance of those services for which the state was invented. Should the civil magistrate carry oppression to such a length that his authority becomes intolerable no one is bound to submit to it. Passive obedience is an absurdity ; the right of resistance is as law-

fully founded as the right to self-preservation. " No nation
that could find any remedy," says Hume, " ever yet suffered
the cruel ravages of a tyrant or were blamed for their
resistance."

At the same time Hume is very careful to point out that
however justifiable the right to resistance may be it cannot
legitimately be invoked except in desperate emergencies. It
is the bounden duty of every one to remember that although
" liberty is the perfection of civil society, *authority is essential
to its very being.*"[1] Before pushing matters to an extremity,
therefore, men ought to ponder well the advantages they
enjoy, and realize that revolutions generally end in the establishment of new and more alarming despotisms. Thus the
old formula *Fiat justitia ruat cælum* is foolish : it sacrifices
the end to the means.

How far Hume was prepared to go in the direction of
supporting established authority will be clear from the
following sentences. " I must confess," he writes,[2] " that
*I shall always incline to their side who draw the bond of allegiance
very close,* and consider an infringement of it as the last
refuge in desperate cases, when the public is in the highest
danger from violence and tyranny. . . . Besides we must
consider that, *as obedience is our duty in the common course
of things, it ought chiefly to be inculcated.*"

We may conclude, then, that Hume had a strong bias
against revolution in general ; that his conception of what
constituted justifiable rebellion would comprise very few
instances in history ; and that the final test of all political
movements, institutions, parties, and policies, is the utility
they confer upon the nation.

To what extent was he guided by these principles in his
treatment of the constitutional crisis of the seventeenth
century ? Did he abandon his philosophical tenets and
" plead the cause of tyranny like an advocate " ? or, was
his verdict simply the outcome of applying political theory
to the facts ? A glance at the History of England will show

[1] Or, " If the reason be asked of that obedience which we are bound to
pay to government, I readily answer, *Because society could not otherwise
subsist.*"—*Of the Original Contract.*
[2] *Of Passive Obedience.*

that there is, on the whole, a fairly close correspondence between the views of the philosopher and those of the historian. The slight divergence which exists is due to the fact that, in handling the situation, he had really two different tests to apply to it—on the one hand the political philosophy already alluded to, and on the other, the general doctrine of utility. The first inclined him to the conservative standpoint and to a purely intellectual appreciation of the facts ; the second, which directed his attention more to the results of the movement than to the theories which supported or opposed it, drove him into the royalist camp. In other words, the excesses committed in the name of justice appalled and repelled him ; he altered his standpoint, and to some extent modified his judgment. It is the operation of this second principle, then, that has occasioned most of the misunderstanding from which Hume has suffered.

In Hume's eyes the original root of the trouble between king and Parliament was not that Charles I laid claim to impossible powers ; but that these powers were, at the time, vague and ill-defined. The Constitution, he contends, at the accession of the House of Stuart, was in a confused state, allowing great authority to the Crown, but resting that authority, not on military force or money, but on public opinion, "influenced by ancient precedent and example." Hence the anxiety of the Stuarts to preserve their prerogative intact was perfectly natural ; for they knew that if the claims they put forward were ravished from them they possessed no other means of maintaining their dignity or of enforcing the laws.[1] History has shown, says Hume, that arbitrary power must reside somewhere in all governments, it being " doubtful whether human society could ever reach that state of perfection as to support itself with no other control than the general and rigid maxims of law and equity."[2] The question, therefore, reduces itself to this : could Charles be entrusted with the balance of arbitrary power in the Constitution ? Parliament thought not ; and Parliament, in Hume's eyes was right.[3] In monarchical constitutions

[1] *History*, Vol. VI, p. 162.   [2] *Ibid.*, p. 421.
[3] *Ibid.*, p. 421.   " The parliament *justly* thought, that the king was too eminent a magistrate to be trusted with discretionary power, which he might

" an eternal jealousy must be preserved against the Sovereign," lest he may turn his great power to the destruction
of liberty.[1] But the point was so fine, and the balance so
difficult to maintain, that trespass in one direction or the
other was, in the nature of things, practically certain. The
fluidity of the Constitution was a temptation and an opportunity to the king to enlarge the sphere of his prerogative,
and at the same time an encouragement to Parliament to
extend its privileges and powers to the detriment of the
monarchical basis of the State. And this is precisely what
happened. Charles " screwed up the springs of government,"
without realizing that the more he did so, unprovided as he
was with sufficient military force to retain them in that
position, the more fatally and violently would they fly out
again when any accident occurred to restore them to their
normal action.[2] He was, in short, " running on a road
surrounded on all sides with the most dangerous precipices,"
and without a plan. On the other hand, the Commons,
" by their unpliableness and independence, were insensibly
changing, perhaps improving, the spirit and genius, while
preserving the form of the Constitution."[3]

If the struggle had continued along constitutional lines
there is little doubt that Hume would have handled it in the
same critical way as he handled all problems, by setting
down the *pros* and *cons* with scrupulous care for exact truth.
And his views as a political philosopher would have determined his judgment on the points at issue. But it is not
possible to discuss revolutions in this way : they never work
themselves out on a basis of abstract right, nor do they
progress logically to a conclusion, in the manner of an argument. Passion supervenes, side-issues intrude themselves,
men forget the object with which they started, and become
blind to all but their immediate aims ; and the result is, that
the final outcome often bears little or no correspondence to

so easily turn to the destruction of liberty. And in the event it has hitherto
been found, that, though some sensible inconveniences arise from the maxim
of adhering strictly to law, yet the advantages overbalance them, and should
render the English grateful to the memory of their ancestors, who, after
repeated contests, at last established that noble, though dangerous principle."

[1] *Ibid.*, p. 160.   [2] *Ibid.*, p. 258.   [3] *Ibid.*, pp. 222-3.

the original cause. Thus while Hume was admirably
equipped for analysing the arguments put forward on behalf
of Crown and Parliament—and did so with lucidity[1]—he
found himself confronted with a situation to which the
niceties of philosophical discussion did not apply. The
" fury of the multitude," the violence and destruction of
accompanying the triumph of the sectaries, the appearance of
a new despotism, which put the tyranny of the Stuarts in the
shade—all this led him to shift the basis of his argument
and to judge the revolution on grounds of utility rather than
of right. It seemed to him that the emergency he had
postulated as the necessary condition prior to an appeal to
extreme measures had never existed ; that this rebellion
was, therefore, wanton, unprincipled, and destructive of the
best interests of the nation. So he condemned the revolution and all its works. Not only so : this antipathy coloured
his attitude to every aspect of it. He even doubted whether
there had been any tyranny at all in England. " Could
human nature," he remarks,[2] " ever reach happiness, the
condition of the English gentry under so mild and benign
a prince, might merit that appellation." It also, as the last
sentence indicates, affected his conception of the king's
character. Charles is " generous," " mild," " virtuous,"
" benevolent," " tolerant " ; he possesses " goodness of
heart " ; his errors are " weaknesses " ; he is pursued by the
malevolence of his enemies to the very night before his death,
when the hammers of workmen erecting the scaffold resound
in his ears. Not a word is uttered of the king's perfidy, which
gained for him the reputation of being the " falsest prince
in Christendom." On the other side of the stage stand the
Puritans—" sanctified hypocrites " who " pollute " their
language with " mysterious jargon," " interlard their iniquities
with long and fervent prayers," are noted for their
sourness and austerity. Their leaders are " ambitious,"
" enthusiastic," " dark, ardent and dangerous," " extra-
vagant," " impetuous," and " violent " ; and their actions
bear the stamp of " dissimulation," " artifice," and " fraud."

[1] E.g. *ibid.*, pp. 246-9.
[2] *Ibid.*, Vol. VI, p. 171.

In fact, there is not a lovable character among them, nor a wholly creditable action.

All this, of course, is far removed from the impartiality with which Hume set out, and it also marks a departure from his original position on the subject of political obligation. But the surprising thing is not that he abandoned his principles : rather it is that he contrived to adhere to them so well. A comparison between the sentences already quoted from the essay on " Passive Obedience " and his final summing up after the execution of the king will show that the difference is one of degree and not of kind. This is the gist of his final remarks :[1] " If ever, on any occasion, it were laudable to conceal truth from the populace, it must be confessed that the doctrine of resistance affords such an example ; and that all speculative reasoners ought to observe, with regard to this principle, the same cautious silence which the laws in every species of government have ever prescribed to themselves. . . . Or, should it be found impossible to restrain the license of human disquisitions, it must be acknowledged that the doctrine of obedience ought alone to be inculcated, and that the exceptions, which are rare, ought seldom or never to be mentioned in popular reasonings and discourses. . . . That illusion, if it be an illusion, which teaches us to pay a sacred regard to the person of princes, is so salutary, that to dissipate it by the formal trial and punishment of a sovereign, will have more pernicious effects upon the people than the example of justice can be supposed to have a beneficial influence upon princes, by checking their career of tyranny."[2]

---

[1] *Ibid.*, Vol. VII, pp. 148-50.

[2] Cf. also Vol. VIII, p. 323 : " The Whig party, for a course of nearly seventy years, has, almost without interruption, enjoyed the whole authority of government ; and no honours or offices could be obtained but by their countenance and protection. But this event, which, in some particulars, has been advantageous to the state, has proved obstructive to the truth of history, and has established many gross falsehoods, which it is unaccountable how any civilized nation could have embraced with regard to its domestic occurrences. . . . *And forgetting that a regard to liberty, though a laudable passion, ought commonly to be subordinate to a reverence for established government, the prevailing faction has celebrated only the partisans of the former, who pursued as their object the perfection of civil society, and has extolled them at the expense of their antagonists, who maintained those maxims that are essential to its very existence.*"

CONCLUSION

All histories, it may be said, must partake of the nature of a narrative ; in fact, narrative is the basic element of historical composition. And the chief formal problem which the historian has to solve is how to assemble and punctuate his narrative so as to render it intelligible, and at the same time not wearisome to the mind of the reader. The old chroniclers achieved this partly by the variety of the matters they related, and partly by the mechanical device of opening and closing their chapters with the accessions and deaths of kings. Voltaire, we have seen, hit upon the plan of breaking up the subject-matter into phases or facets of the period he happened to be handling, and of examining each in turn as a more or less self-contained unit. Hume belonged both to the old dispensation and to the new. In general, he worked on the old chronicle plan of writing history by reigns, and confining his attention solely to political events ; but from time to time he suspends the even flow of his narrative to gather up, after the manner, though without the distinction, of Voltaire, the non-political features of each period before embarking upon fresh material.[1] The difference between the two historians in this particular is noteworthy. Voltaire's chapters on *mœurs* are among his most brilliant ; Hume's register his most signal failure. To the modern mind, they exhibit no vestige of order or connexion ; on the contrary, they are merely chaotic catalogues of casually-selected facts dealing with social and economic phenomena, literature, or uncommon occurrences, which have struck the author in the course of his reading : rag-bags, as it were, specifically invented to receive whatever odds and ends cannot be utilized in the main body of the history. The quantity of information thus packed away is, perhaps, a testimony to the care with which Hume selected his chief *data* ; but it is also, unfortunately, a reflection on the extreme narrowness of his outlook as a historian. In any case, little,

[1] *Vide* Vol. I, pp. 197-229 ; Vol. II, pp. 101-42 ; Vol. V, pp. 451-92 ; Vol. VI, pp. 157-98.

if any, advantage can be drawn from these curious chapters. The *History of England*, however, displays a much more striking flaw, and one less to be condoned. It is only too patent that frequently the main narrative itself breaks down from lack of power or insight on the part of the author to integrate the facts he has assembled. Again and again the reader comes across phrases like these : " The following are the most important laws passed during this reign," or simply : " Miscellaneous transactions of this reign," which are nothing more nor less than formulas of despair, indications of incomplete assimilation.[1]

But after all the damnatory criticism has been passed, and all the omissions, errors, and misconceptions have been listed, it cannot be said that Hume as a historian has been completely demolished and discredited. The value of history does not lie in the multiplicity of correct facts it contains ; nor are all facts, however correctly ascertained and articulated, of the same worth—links in a chain of equal strength and importance. There are major and minor occurrences, periods when history reaches a crisis or peak, and periods, again, when it lapses into the drab and commonplace ; and although it is necessary to search out the minor events in order to comprehend properly the significance of the major, nevertheless the ethical values of the great occurrences stand on a plane by themselves. Criticisms of capital importance may be passed upon them even if the writer has only an imperfect idea of their antecedents. Thus, Hume's moralizing on the death of Charles I, or his remarks on the Reformation in England, or, indeed, any of the great historical events he dealt with, have a value that does not stale with age. They read as freshly to-day as when they were first penned, and there are many students, both inside and outside the professional ranks, who still find them satisfying and illuminating. The wonderful ease, directness, and perspicuity of the style in which they are expressed, together with the depth, wisdom, and concentrated experience distilled into them, make them, as Hume hoped they would be, " instructive and amusing " in the highest degree.

[1] Vol. I, p. 464 ; II, pp. 35, 222, 319, 361, 486 ; III, pp. 118, 212, 397, etc.

ROBERTSON

ROBERTSON'S *History of Scotland,* with which he ushered in his celebrated series of masterpieces, burst upon the reading public with the *éclat* of a prodigy. It was hardly to be expected that another post of honour in the English Parnassus of history would fall to a compatriot of David Hume. But the surprise soon passed into admiration when the virtues of the new historian became apparent. "There is a history lately come out," writes Lord Chesterfield,[1] "of the reign of Mary Queen of Scots and King James her son, written by one Robertson a Scotsman, which for clearness, purity, and dignity of style I will not scruple to compare with the best historians extant, not excepting Davila, Guicciardini, and perhaps Livy." Horace Walpole and Gibbon were no less complimentary in their references. "The perfect composition, the nervous language, the well-turned periods of Dr. Robertson," writes the latter,[2] "inflamed me to the ambitious hope that I might one day tread in his foot-steps." And Lord Lyttleton is credited with the astounding remark, that there had scarcely been a better writer "since the time of St. Paul!"[3]

It is not easy for the modern mind to account for the torrent of eulogy poured out on Robertson, either in this country or on the Continent.[4] He has none of Voltaire's brilliance, or Hume's philosophic depth, or Gibbon's incisive learning; on the contrary, he is often ponderous, prolix, and sententious, and his slow acumen places a strain on the attention of the reader. If we exclude, for the moment, the more purely narrative parts of his histories, which have great merit

[1] *Letters to his Son,* Apl. 16, 1759.
[2] *Autobiography* (ed. G. B. Hill), p. 122.
[3] D. Stewart : *Life of Robertson,* p. 119.
[4] "C'est à vous et à M. Hume qu'il appartient d' écrire l'histoire. Vous êtes éloquent, savant, et impartiel."—(Voltaire to Robertson, 26 Feb., 1778).— *Œuvres,* XLVI, p. 574.

it may be said with confidence that he invariably speaks like an academician, in cap and gown, with all the solemnity of one who is accustomed to be taken *au pied de la lettre*, and cannot afford to be mistaken.　There is no possibility that the reader will find any sparkle, or enthusiasm, or exuberance in his books : he is consistently sober, balanced, restrained ; and contrives, either by accident or design, to diffuse over his text a certain tonelessness, which resembles nothing so much as the appearance of his beloved Edinburgh under the grey caress of an east wind.　At the same time the purity of his diction is incontestable, and its very sobriety imparts to it a dignity, which Edmund Burke[1] and others found much superior to the *falsetto* and " word-catching " of Gibbon.　In all probability his popularity as a writer arose from the fact that he had discovered a medium of literary expression, which combined the precision due to history with perfect decorum, dignity, and correctness.[2]

But when full allowance has been made for literary art the impression Robertson creates depends primarily on his accuracy and general truthfulness.　Like Gibbon, he professed himself to be a careful scholar, intent upon the discovery of truth, and anxious above all things to convey it to his readers without distortion or abbreviation.　" To relate real occurrences, and to explain their real causes and effects," he once remarked,[3] " is the historian's peculiar and only province."　Again,[4] " The longer I reflect on the nature of historical composition," he says, " the more I am convinced that scrupulous accuracy is necessary.　The historian who records the events of his own times, is credited in proportion to the opinion which the public entertains with respect to his means of information, and his veracity.　He who delineates the transactions of a remote period, has no title to claim assent, unless he produces evidence in proof of his

---

[1] D. Stewart : *Life of Robertson*, pp. 229-30, note.

[2] " The style seems pompous and stilted to us now, for it belongs to a formal age of cocked hats, knee-breeches, and bag-wigs. Possessed of a profound sense of the Majesty of History, the author approaches her in court costume, and addresses her with ceremony."—Graham : *Scottish Men of Letters in the XVIIIth Century*, p. 98.

[3] *History of Scotland*, Bk. II, p. 180.

[4] *History of America*, Preface.

assertions. Without this, he may write an amusing tale,
but he cannot be said to have composed an authentic history."
The same spirit animates the sentences with which he closes
his inquiry into the manners and customs of the American
Indians : [1] " In this I aspire not at rivalling the great masters
who have painted and adorned savage life, either in boldness
of design, or in the glow and beauty of their colouring. I am
satisfied with the more humble merit of having persisted with
patient industry in viewing my subject in many various lights,
and collecting from the most accurate observers such detached
and often minute features, as might enable me to exhibit a
portrait that resembles the original."

Robertson's anxiety to secure factual accuracy was indeed
unquenchable ; he was prepared to put himself to any
amount of trouble to unearth information, or to track a
matter to its source—a quality all the more admirable in one
who spent his life amid the cares and distractions of a parish
clergyman and the exacting routine duties of a university
principal. It was an age, moreover, when the researcher
frequently found his way blocked by the inaccessibility of
archives, or the selfishness of those who owned the indispensable documents. But the perseverence of Robertson
triumphed over most difficulties, or he found a way of circum-
venting them. The preparation of his first history—the
History of Scotland—was comparatively plain sailing ; there
was a plethora of material to hand which, he tells us,[2] would
have satisfied the most exacting antiquary. The great
Cottonian collection, embodying the Cecil papers, had been
ransacked by a number of industrious investigators—Digges,
Anderson, Keith, Haynes, and Forbes—and the results of
their labours were, for the most part, in print. But Robertson
was not content with printed *data* ; with the true instinct
of the researcher he sought out the unpublished and the
inédit. Thus he consulted original MSS. in the Advocates'
Library, Edinburgh, and in the British Museum, and borrowed
private papers in the possession of Lord Royston, Sir David
Dalrymple, and others. Nothing like so massive a " domes-

---

[1] *History of America*, Bk. IV, p. 397.
[2] *History of Scotland*, Preface.

day " of material had ever been compassed by any previous historian ; and when it was presented to the reading public of Great Britain in limpid prose there was no room for doubt that a new epoch had begun in Scottish historiography.

He was not always so fortunate in the collection of material. When he undertook to write the *History of America*, some years later, he found himself confronted with obstacles that might well have cut short his progress and caused him to abandon the task. Almost all his *data* lay in Spain and had to be procured through the help of intermediaries ; for a prolonged visit to the Peninsula was impossible. Moreover, the Spanish Government increased his troubles by jealously guarding its *Archivo* at Simancas from the eye of the researcher, and by charging excessive fees for the privilege of copying documents from those who were fortunate enough to obtain a permit to consult them. Nevertheless, with the assistance of Lord Grantham, British ambassador at Madrid, and a certain Mr. Waddilove, chaplain to the Embassy, he managed to acquire a valuable collection of documents, chronicles, and histories by purchase from Spanish book-sellers, and with this as his foundation proceeded to build up the first authentic and readable history of Spanish America. Sir Murray Keith procured him copies of original letters dealing with Cortez' expedition to Mexico, together with examples of Mexican paintings, from the Imperial Library of Vienna. From St. Petersburg, again, by the friendly help of the Empress Catherine, a keen admirer of *Charles V*, came an interesting original document, in the shape of Captain Krenitzin's voyage of exploration in the Behring Sea, by means of which he was able to broach the then novel theory that America was probably populated from N.E. Asia. The Portuguese ambassador in London supplied him with valuable information regarding the character and institutions of the Indians of Brazil ; M. Suard, his French translater, intro-duced him to Frenchmen who had resided in both North and South America ; Protestant missionaries gave him similar details about the habits of the Indians of the Five Nations. Finally, from Alexander Dalrymple he obtained the perusal of two volumes of manuscript memorials dealing with the internal organizations of the Spanish colonies during the reigns of Philip III and Philip IV.[1] All this varied information Robertson carefully digested and checked, paying the greatest possible attention to the credibility of his various sources. The care with which he worked is shown in the copiousness of his notes, references, and citations, in his enumeration and scrutiny of his authorities, and in the habit he cultivated of pressing back to the *ipsissima verba* of the actors and eyewitnesses, if such were obtainable.

Robertson's scholarship is visible, again, in the considerable degree of detachment he attained—considerable, that is, for the age in which he lived. It is true, of course, that he adopted many of the words and phrases of the *Enlightenment* ; he could not avoid doing so, since they formed the substratum of every one's vocabulary. He was likewise limited by the general intellectual outlook of his contemporaries. Thus, for example, he speaks with all the freedom, if not the nauseating repetition, of Hume of " enthusiasm," " frenzy," " fanaticism," and " superstition " ; he treats Catholicism as a species of " false " religion, and scholasticism as a vain, metaphysical, and frivolous subtlety ; and he despises the mystical experiences of Ignatius Loyola as beneath the notice of a serious historian. It would appear, too, that he grossly exaggerated the " darkness " of the Middle Ages. In his examination of certain passages in the first volume of *Charles V*, S. R. Maitland has shown conclusively [2] that Robertson's facts were very exiguous ; that his conclusions were biased ; that he was sometimes guilty of misreading his authorities, and even, on occasion, of misrepresenting them ; that he had the unhistorical habit of combining evidence derived from different centuries ; and that he did not always grasp the significance of the facts he adduced in support of his judgments. Nevertheless, when the necessary deductions have been made on these various heads, and it is borne in mind that Robertson's interest in mediaeval history was merely incidental, the degree of objectivity with which he wrote is remarkable. He perceived clearly the civilizing

[1] *History of America*, Preface.
[2] *The Dark Ages*, pp. 33-9, 54-7, 66-72, 75, 79, 86, 130-5, 169-75.

work of the Church—the humanitarianism of the clergy in furthering the manumission of serfs,[1] and in alleviating some of the worst evils of feudalism by the institution of the *Treuga Dei*.[2] He observed also the beneficial effects of the Canon Law in mollifying and improving the fierce barbaric justice of the secular courts,[3] and the positive results of the Crusades, despite the " frenzy " that gave birth to them.[4] He can even find an appreciative word for the work of the Jesuit Order.[5] When he comes to deal with the Reformation his superiority over Hume, for instance, is still more marked ; for, instead of explaining away the movement as the more or less accidental outcome of non-spiritual forces and the happy play of chance occurrences, he gives it a moral as well as a political setting and justifies the argument of the Reformers.[6] His picture of Luther, although by no means flattering, is marked by sympathy, and is certainly not unjust.[7] He sees him as an arrogant, impetuous, obstinate, and sometimes scurrilous popular leader ; but at the same time a man of undaunted courage, unwearied industry, superior to considerations of self, and the exponent of an austere and simple virtue. His vices, moreover, he notes are the defects of his qualities, chargeable not to the malevolence of his disposition, but to the manners of the age. In other words, Robertson's Luther displays many features of a great and heroic character.

The same criticism might be passed on all the pen-portraits that adorn the pages of his histories : they are drawn without exaggeration or malice, even if the principles for which the individuals stood, and the policy they followed, do not meet with his approval. The mirror which he held up to nature may not reflect with all the brightness and sharpness of Voltaire's ; but there is never any doubt as to the main lines of the physiognomies represented in it ; and, above all, there are no caricatures or gross misconceptions. He is the most impeccable of eighteenth century historians. Take, for

---

[1] *A View of the State of Europe*, etc., Sect. I, p. 66, note.
[2] *Ibid.*, pp. 72-3, and note, p. 76.
[3] *Ibid.*, pp. 101-2.
[4] *Ibid.*, pp. 45-50.
[5] *Ibid.*, pp. 119-20.
[6] *Charles V*, Bk. II, p. 326 *et seq.*
[7] *Ibid.*, Bk. VIII, pp. 192-5.

instance, his description of Mary of Lorraine, the Scottish Regent (1544–49), whom Knox calumniated. " No princess," he remarks,[1] " ever possessed qualities more capable of rendering her administration illustrious or the kingdom happy. Of much discernment, and no less address ; of great intrepidity and equal prudence ; gentle and humane without weakness ; zealous for her religion without bigotry ; a lover of justice without rigour. One circumstance, however, and that, too, the excess of a virtue, rather than any vice, poisoned all these great qualities, and rendered her government unfortunate and her name odious. Devoted to the interest of France, her native country, and attached to the princes of Lorraine, her brothers, with most passionate fondness, she departed, in order to gratify them, from every maxim which her widsom or humanity would have approved. . . . But, even by her enemies, these unjustifiable actions were imputed to the facility, not the malignity of her nature ; and while they taxed her brothers and French counsellors with rashness and cruelty, they still allowed her the praise of prudence and lenity."

Perhaps Robertson's objectivity is most distinctly noticeable in the purely narrative parts of his histories. Here, indeed, he stands on a plane by himself in the eighteenth century. " The things described," writes Lord Brougham,[2] " are presented in the clearest light and with the most vivid and unambitious colouring, without exaggeration and apparently without effort." He was temperamentally averse to ornamental, picturesque, or imaginative flights, as dangerous to that factual exactness, which it was his prime endeavour to achieve ; and, as a rule, he keeps very close to his authorities. His models were Swift and Defoe—the two writers who are generally held to have realized most nearly the ideal of pure prose diction. Read *Robinson Crusoe*, he once advised a brother professor, who was struggling with the difficulties of expression, and if this does not help you, try *Gulliver's Travels*.[3] The virtues of Robertson's descriptive

[1] *History of Scotland*, Bk. III, pp. 210-11.
[2] *Lives of Men of Letters and Science in the Time of George III*, p. 281.
[3] *Ibid.*, p. 304.

style will became more apparent if we take two examples, and compare them with the efforts of other writers who covered the same ground. Consider, for instance, the following account of the discovery of America as given in the pages of Robertson.[1] After noting the fact that, for some days, Columbus had been convinced that an early landfall was practically certain, he proceeds :

From all these symptoms, Columbus was so confident of being near land, that on the evening of the 11th October, after public prayers for success, he ordered the sails to be furled, and the ships to lie to, keeping strict watch, lest they should be driven ashore in the night. During this interval of suspense and expectation, no man shut his eyes, all kept upon deck, gazing intently towards that quarter where they expected to discover the land which had been so long the object of their wishes. About two hours after midnight, Columbus standing on the forecastle, observed a light at a distance, and privately pointed it out to Pedro Guttierez, a page of the Queen's wardrobe. Guttierez perceived it and calling to Salcedo, comptroller of the fleet, all three saw it in motion, as if it were carried from place to place. A little after midnight the joyful sound of Land ! Land ! was heard from the *Pinta* which kept always ahead of the other ships. But having been so often deceived by fallacious appearances, every man was now become slow of belief and waited in all the anguish of uncertainty and impatience for the return of day. As soon as morning dawned, all doubts and fears were dispelled. From every ship an island was seen about two leagues to the north, whose flat and verdant fields, well stored with wood, and watered with many rivulets, presented the aspect of a delightful country.

There are, of course, errors in this account, due to the fact that the Journal of Columbus was not discovered until 1791, and Robertson had to depend for his details on the *Life* given in Churchill's *Voyages*. For example, the sails were not ordered to be furled until 2 a.m. *when the land was seen* ; Guttierez was not a page of the Queen's wardrobe, but overseer of the King's bed-chamber ; Salcedo should be Roderigo Sanchez of Segovia ; the " forecastle " should be the

---

[1] *History of America*, Bk. II, pp. 102-3.

"poop"; the light observed was not "carried from place to place," but "like a taper, now high now low"; and it was Columbus who summoned Sanchez, not Guttierez. But apart from these mistakes as to fact the description is masterly in its simplicity, dignity, and restraint. As Lord Brougham points out, the word "verdant" is probably the only false note : it is unnecessary.

Turn now to the more glowing and picturesque account given of the same event in the pages of Washington Irving's *Life of Columbus* :[1]

The greatest animation prevailed throughout the ships : not an eye was closed that night. As the evening darkened Columbus took his station on the top of the castle or cabin on the high poop of his vessel. However he might carry a cheerful and confident countenance during the day, it was to him a time of most painful anxiety ; and now, when he was *wrapped from observation by the shades of night*, he maintained an intense and unremitting watch, *ranging his eye along the dusky horizon in search of the most vague indications of land. Suddenly*, about two o'clock he thought he beheld a light glimmering at a distance. Fearing that his eager hopes might deceive him he called to Pedro Guttierez, gentleman of the King's bed-chamber, and demanded whether he saw a light in that direction : the latter *replied in the affirmative*. Columbus, yet doubtful whether it might not be some delusion of the fancy, called Rodrigo Sanchez of Segovia, and made the same inquiry. By the time the latter had ascended the round house the light had disappeared. They saw it once or twice afterwards in sudden and passing gleams, *as if it were a torch on the bark of a fisherman, rising and sinking with the waves ; or in the hands of some person on shore, borne up and down as he walked from house to house. . . .*

The thoughts and feelings of Columbus in this little space of time must have been tumultuous and intense. At length, in spite of every difficulty and danger, he had accomplished his object. The great mystery of the ocean was revealed ; his theory, which had been the scoff of sages, was triumphantly established ; *he had secured to himself a glory which must be as durable as the world itself*, etc., etc.

How tawdry much of this seems when placed beside the

[1] T. Nelson & Sons, 1844.

simple and direct description of Robertson. The words in italics will be sufficient to indicate where the difference lies between the two styles. Irving, not satisfied with the plain record given by Columbus, must needs touch it up for the consumption of the general reader : as a journalist works up " copy " for a sensational article in a newspaper. Robertson, on the other hand, with an eye on the *things* he is describing rather than on the sentiments that arise in his own mind, merely relates the facts, and trusts to their novelty to supply the dramatic element. Considered simply as literature, and apart altogether from the history involved, there can really be no comparison between the two narratives. No one but a rhetorician would, for example, describe Columbus as seeing a light " suddenly," or, as " ranging his eye along the *dusky* horizon " ; for, in point of fact, it is the nature of lights to be seen suddenly at night, and of horizons, in the evening, to be dusky. But perhaps the weakest part of Irving's account is where he makes Guttierez answer Columbus " in the affirmative," as if, for all the world, he were a modern Cabinet minister.

The discovery of Mexico is another occasion where the simplicity of Robertson stands out to great advantage against the more picturesque descriptions of subsequent writers. Compare, for example, the accounts given in Robertson and Prescott of the actual moment when Cortes and his men came into view of the vale of Mexico. Robertson, as usual, keeps close to the record—in this case, the chronicle of Bernal Diaz del Castillo, who accompanied the expedition in the capacity of a simple soldier ; and his story runs as follows : [1]

In descending from the mountains of Chalco, across which the road lay, the vast plain of Mexico opened gradually to their view. When they first beheld this prospect, one of the most striking and beautiful on the face of the earth ; when they observed fertile and cultivated fields, stretching farther than the eye could reach ; when they saw a lake resembling the sea in extent, encompassed with large towers, and discovered the capital city rising upon an island in the middle, adorned with its

[1] *History of America*, Bk. V, pp. 446-7.

temples and turrets ; the scene so far exceeded their imagination, that some believed the fanciful descriptions of romance were realized, and that its enchanted palaces and gilded domes were presented to their sight ; others could hardly persuade themselves that this wonderful spectacle was anything more than a dream. As they advanced, their doubts were removed, but their amazement increased. They were now fully satisfied that the country was rich beyond any conception which they had formed of it, and flattered themselves that at length they should obtain an ample recompense for all their services and sufferings.

Now take Prescott's narrative : [1]

They had not advanced far, when, turning an angle of the sierra, they suddenly came on a view which more than compensated the toils of the preceding day. It was that of the valley of Mexico, or Tenochtitlan, as more commonly called by the natives, which, *with its picturesque assemblage of water, woodland, and cultivated plains, its shining cities and shadowy hills*, was spread out like some gay and gorgeous panorama before them. *In the highly rarified atmosphere of these upper regions, even remote objects have a brilliancy of colouring and a distinctness of outline which seem to annihilate distance.* Stretching far away at their feet were seen noble forests of oak, sycamore, and cedar, and beyond, yellow fields of maize and the towering maguey, intermingled with orchards and blooming gardens : *for flowers, in such demand for their religious festivals, were more abundant in this populous valley than in other parts of Anahuac.* In the centre of the great basin were beheld the lakes, occupying then a much larger portion of its surface than at present ; their borders thickly studded with towers and hamlets, and, in the midst— *like some Indian Empress with her coronal of pearls*—the fair city of Mexico, with her white towers and pyramidal temples, reposing, as it were, on the bosom of the waters—*the far-famed " Venice of the Aztecs."* . . . *It was like the spectacle which greeted the eyes of Moses from the summit of Pisgah,* and in the warm glow of their feelings, they cried out, " It is the Promised Land."

Prescott's art is undoubted. He could decorate a blank panel in the vast and void of the past with the hand of a master ; and no one would imagine, from the intimacy of the description, that he had never visited the scenery he

[1] *The Conquest of Mexico*, Bk. III, Chap. VIII.

portrays.[1] Compared with the plain homespun of Robertson, his diction and imagery are impressive to the last degree. Yet, of the two accounts, Robertson's is the more valuable, historically, because it practically reproduces a first-hand document, and gives all the features which the eye of the Spaniard actually took in. Prescott's is, by contrast, essentially a subjective effusion. Excise the italicized passages, which are really importations and have no basis in contemporary documents, and the superiority of Robertson will become clear at a glance.

HIS GENERAL POINT OF VIEW AS A HISTORIAN

Robertson's standpoint as a historian, as we should expect, bears a generic resemblance to that of Voltaire, Hume, and the philosophical school generally ; like them, he regarded history not as a record of fact so much as a *corpus* of instruction, a teacher of wisdom, for the benefit of the statesman and the philosopher. From which it follows that he shows a similar disinclination to dwell on those periods of history when public transactions are either wrapped in obscurity or afford little instruction. In his opinion such periods ought to be totally neglected by the serious student, or " abandoned to the industry and credulity of the antiquary." [2] " Nations as well as men," he avers, " arrive at maturity by degrees, and the events which happened during their infancy or early youth, cannot be recollected, and *deserve not to be remembered*." [3] In a sense, Robertson's antipathy to history that could not be authenticated by documents is stronger than Hume's ; for it is a patent fact that he was never tempted into writing a detailed account of the Middle Ages. He begins his Scottish history, properly speaking, with the birth of Mary Stuart (1542), and compresses all he thinks vital in previous centuries into some sixty-three pages. Likewise his *Charles V* is, as it professes to be, primarily the history of certain aspects of public events during the six-

[1] He was largely dependent upon Humboldt.—*Essai Politique sur le Royaume de Nouvelle Espagne.*
[2] *History of Scotland*, Bk. I, p. 42.   [3] *Ibid.*, p. 39.

teenth century ; and the whole sweep of mediaeval history is curtailed to the narrow compass of a prefatory essay. This does not mean, of course, that Robertson was perfunctory in his attitude to the Middle Ages, or that he regarded them with contempt. On the contrary, he was much more careful and scientific in his investigations, such as they were, than either of his contemporaries. The real difference betweeh him and the modern historian is that he was not prepared to treat mediaeval history as an end in itself ; its value and importance, to him, lay entirely in the fact that it was a period of preparation, when the institutions with which we are now familiar took their rise and grew to maturity. In other words, instead of being a negative epoch or back-water in human affairs, the Middle Ages were characterized by progress ; their key-note, in Robertson's opinion, was development. Accordingly, the function of the historian who dips into their obscurities is not to spend time over minute inquiries into origins—though, up to a point, this is necessary—but to keep his eye steadily fixed on the goal towards which events and tendencies were making, and to describe the past in the light of this. Thus his *View of the State of Europe*, prefixed to *Charles V* is not a history in the strict sense of the word, but a philosophic survey—a record, not of events, but of forces and influences ; a kind of physiological analysis of the developing structure of European civilization, akin in spirit to Montesquieu's *Grandeur et Decadence des Romains*. " It is necessary," he says,[1] " to mark the great steps by which they [i.e. the nations of Europe] advanced from barbarism to refinement, and to point out those general principles and events which, by their uniform as well as extensive operation, conducted all of them to that degree of improvement in policy and in manners which they had attained at the period when Charles V began his reign." And again,[2] " In pointing out and explaining these causes and events, it is not necessary to observe the order of time with a chronological accuracy ; it is of more importance to keep in view their mutual connexion and dependence, and to show how the operation of one event, or one cause, prepared the

[1] *View of the State of Europe*, Sec. I, p. 21.   [2] *Ibid.*, p. 40.

way for another, and augmented its influence." The same broad principle holds good also of Book I in the first volume of the *History of Scotland*; it is not an account of mediaeval Scottish history, but an analysis of the chief factors that co-operated together in the production of the State and of society, as they stood at the commencement of modern times. Thus he divides Scottish history into four periods: [1] from the origin of the monarchy to the reign of Kenneth II; from Kenneth II's conquest of the Picts to the death of Alexander III; from the death of Alexander III to the death of James V; and from the death of James V to the Union of the crowns. The first two periods are either entirely fabulous and conjectural and have no interest for the historian, or require only to be "slightly touched." With the third begins the authentic record, and this period deserves to be read and *studied* by "every Scotsman." But it is the fourth that he proposes to deal with in detail, because Scotland now enters into the general life of Christendom, and her history has an interest not only to Scotsmen but to foreigners as well. Without further apology, therefore, he concentrates the preliminary attention of his readers on the main events of interest in the great formative epoch 1286–1542.

The comprehensiveness of these surveys, the skill and insight displayed in marshalling the relevant facts, the eminent wisdom of the deductions drawn, and the wonderful ease with which the multifarious activities of centuries are brought within the scope of one unified plan—all this renders the first volume of *Charles V*, and in a lesser degree the introductory chapter of the *History of Scotland*, masterpieces of analytical writing. "In surveying the general stream of human events," writes Alison, [2] "and drawing just conclusions regarding the changes of centuries, he was truly admirable; and in those respects his first volume of *Charles V*, may, if we except Guizot's *Civilisation Européene*, be pronounced without a parallel in the whole annals of literature."

The general assumption, then, on which Robertson's

---

[1] *History of Scotland*, Bk. I, p. 42.
[2] *Essays Political, Historical, and Miscellaneous*, Vol. III, p. 420; also p. 81.

attitude rests is that the instructive part of history begins
with the sixteenth century. He regards this period as a
great cross-roads or junction, where the moulding and
shaping forces, operating in Europe for a thousand years,
debouch, so to speak, on the broad highway of modern times.
The national consciousness of European peoples had now
reached a maximum point, the power of the Crown had
asserted itself in all countries to the destruction, or at all
events, the repression, of a licentious feudalism, and all
States " were formed into one great political system." " It is
necessary," he remarks,[1] " not only for those who are called
to conduct the affairs of nations, but for such as inquire and
reason concerning them, to remain satisfied with a general
knowledge of distant events, and to confine their study of
history in detail chiefly to that period in which the several
states of Europe having become intimately connected, the
operations of one power are so felt by all, as to influence
their councils, and to regulate their measures."

In the next place, Robertson was the begetter of the
doctrine known as the " dignity of history." What he meant
by the phrase was not merely that history should be written
in a dignified manner, but principally that it should be
written about dignified events and characters. In a sense,
therefore, it is simply a variant of the maxims laid down by
Voltaire and Hume regarding the selection of *data*, and the
subject-matter with which the historian ought to concern
himself. The broad effect of the doctrine, at any rate, was
similar. It tended to rule out many facts altogether as too
trivial to be noticed by history, to skim lightly over others
as more or less negligible, and to concentrate almost entirely
on those transactions which necessarily demand attention
because of their inherent interest, or because of the instruction to be derived from them. Take, for example, the treatment meted out to Loyola, the founder of the Jesuit Order.
" The wild adventures and visionary schemes in which his
enthusiasm engaged him," says Robertson,[2] " equal anything
recorded in the legends of the Roman Saints, but are *unworthy
of notice in history*." How, then, we may ask, are we to

[1] *Charles V.*, Preface.   [2] *Charles V.*, Bk. VI, p. 111.

understand the motives which led to the foundation of the Society of Jesus ? Apparently we need not trouble about such matters at all ; for, according to Robertson, the ordinary motives of all worldly action will supply a sufficient basis of explanation. Thus he proceeds : " Prompted by this fanatical spirit, or incited by the love of power and distinction, from which such pretenders to superior sanctity are not exempt, Loyola was ambitious of becoming the founder of a religious order." Is it not clear that in this generalized explanation, assuming it to be otherwise correct, he has missed the point ? One might as well try to explain the foundation of the Franciscan movement without reference to the mystical experiences of St. Francis as attempt to understand the origin of the Jesuit Order without some comprehension of the character and outlook of Loyola. The clue is to be found in those very " wild adventures and visionary schemes " which Robertson treated with contempt as unworthy the notice of history. Or, take the passage where he introduces Rizzio into his Scottish history : it begins with a characteristic apology for the descent from the august to the trivial.[1] " The low birth and indigent condition of this man placed him in a station in which he ought naturally to have remained unknown to posterity. But what fortune called him to act and to suffer in Scotland *obliges history to descend from its dignity*, and to record his adventures." What need was there to " descend " ? The reason for devoting attention to any character or event in history lies not so much in the character or event itself as in the place it occupies in the general sequence of cause and effect. Rizzio is worthy of notice, in the last resort, not because of his birth or station, but because of the terrible catastrophe he was instrumental in bringing on the queen. Robertson, of course, realized this ; but he admitted Rizzio to the stage, as it were, only under protest. He would have preferred to keep him out of the action altogether.

There is another way in which the doctrine of the dignity of history exercises an important influence on the handling of facts : it encourages the historian to look askance on circumstantial detail as matter of inferior grade and texture,

---

[1] *History of Scotland*, Bk. III, p. 284.

and to suppress it wherever possible. It will not, for instance,
allow of a story being told for its own sake—grimly, humor-
ously, ironically, pathetically, or satirically, as the case may
be ; but insists upon the maintenance of a high level of
gravity, decorum, and seriousness. The point will perhaps
be clearer if the account given by Robertson of Rizzio's
assassination be set side by side with that given in one of the
contemporary documents on which he relied. In the document [1] the material part of the event is described as follows :

Upon Saturday at night near VIII of the clock the King
conveyeth himself, the Lord Ruthen, George Duglass, and two
others, *through his own chamber by the privy stairs up to the
Queen's chamber, going to which there is a cabinet about XII feet
square ; in the same a little low reposing bed and a table*, at which
there were sitting at the supper the Queen, the Lady Argyll, and
David *with his cap on his head*. Into the cabinet there cometh
in the King and Lord Ruthen, who willed David to come forth,
saying, that this was no place for him. The Queen said that it
was her will. Her husband answered, that it was against her
honour. The Lord Ruthen said, that he should learn better his
duty, and offering to have taken him by the arm, David *took the
Queen by the blychtes of her gown*, and put himself behind the
Queen who would gladly have saved him : but *the King having
loosed his hand, and holding her in his arms, David was thrust out
of the Cabinet through the bed-chamber into the Chamber of presence*
where were the Lords Morton, Lord Lindsey, who intending that
night to have reserved him, and the next day to hang him, so
many being about him, that bore him evil will, one thrust him
into the body with a dagger, and after him a great many others,
so that he had in his body above * * wounds. *It is told for certain,
that the King's dagger was left sticking in him.* . . .
Her husband this time speaketh little, herself continually
weepeth. The Lord Ruthen *being ill at ease and weak calleth
for a drink*, and saith, " This I must do with your Majesty's
pardon," and persuadeth her in the best sort he could, that she
would pacify herself. Nothing that could be said could please
her."

Now observe how Robertson manipulates the facts so as to

[1] Quoted by Robertson : *History of Scotland*, Bk. IV, p. 319 note.

preserve the dignity of his subject. In the first place he carefully ignores the italicized parts, which supply the circumstantial element, and have the effect of lowering the level of the narrative to that of a common murder ; and in the second place he softens, heightens, and generalizes the whole episode, giving it a classical pose alien to the essentially barbaric nature of its accompaniments. These adjustments made, Robertson's version runs thus : [1]

> On the 9th March, Morton entered the court of the palace with a hundred and sixty men ; and without noise, or meeting with any resistance, seized all the gates. While the queen was at supper with the Countess of Argyll, Rizio, and a few other persons, the King suddenly entered the apartment by a private passage. At his back was Ruthven, clad in complete armour, and with that ghastly and horrid look which long sickness had given him. Three or four of his most trusty accomplices followed him. Such an unusual appearance alarmed those who were present. Rizio instantly apprehended that he was the victim at whom the blow was aimed ; and in the utmost consternation retired behind the Queen, of whom he laid hold, hoping that the reverence due to her person might prove some protection to him. The conspirators had proceeded too far to be restrained by any consideration of that kind. Numbers of armed men rushed into the chamber. Ruthven drew his dagger, and with furious mien and voice commanded Rizio to leave a place of which he was unworthy, and which he had occupied too long. Mary employed tears, and entreaties, and threatenings, to save her favourite. But, notwithstanding all these, he was torn from her by violence, and before he could be dragged through the next apartment, the rage of his enemies put an end to his life, piercing his body with fifty-six wounds.

The only realistic touch in this description is Ruthven's " ghastly and horrid look " ; it imparts a certain ruthless grimness to the proceedings. Tytler was so impressed with its artistic value that he embodied the phrase almost word for word in his larger history.[2] But, on the whole, the dignity imposed on the narrative deprives it of the vitalizing power of circumstantial detail.

[1] *Ibid.*, pp. 318-19.   [2] *History of Scotland*, Chap. XIV.

So far we have dwelt on the hampering effect of the doctrine of historical dignity. But it is well to recognize that if it tended to prevent the proper appreciation and use of detail, it kept the historian's eye firmly fixed on the great events and characters, and away from the trivial, the frivolous, and the irrelevant. There is never any danger that Robertson will lose himself in the accumulation of insignificant detail. He holds a straight course through the centre of the period he happens to be engaged upon ; and this, after all, is no mean achievement.

The extension of Robertson's activities as a historian from Scotland to Europe, and from Europe to America—an extension that rendered his reputation abroad more distinguished than Hume's—not only widened his grasp of history, but also deepened his perception of the manifold inquiries a historian must include in his investigations. His power of adaptability, however, was great, and his mind responded to the studies devolved upon it without the slightest difficulty or apparent strain. His researches in American history compelled him to come to close quarters with the manners, customs, and institutions of the Indians, the climate and geography of the American continent, and speculations as to how it was populated—subjects on which the available information was both scattered and confused, as well as scanty. Similarly, his inquiries into the relations between Europe and Asia in ancient and mediaeval times [1] led him to an appreciation of the economic factor in world history, and resulted in a valuable contribution to a type of historical study only beginning to be understood in the eighteenth century.

It cannot be said, however, that the sections in the *History of America* dealing with the aborigines are of equal worth and interest with the rest of the work. [2] In spite of the obvious care devoted to them they seem unreal, mechanical, and unconvincing. The fault probably lay partly in the nature of the matter discussed, and partly in the author himself. It was futile to attempt a comprehensive account

[1] *An Historical Disquisition Concerning the Knowledge which the Ancients had of India*, etc.
[2] *Vide* Bk. IV, pp. 283-401.

of aboriginal customs until the evidence had been properly
collected, sifted, and arranged by competent ethnologists.
Moreover, the ground covered in the survey was too vast to
allow of useful generalizations being made. Even Montesquieu might well have lost himself in the variations of
Patagonian, Carib, and Iroquois customs ; and he was
infinitely better qualified for a task of this sort than Robertson.
The unphilosophical character of the latter's mind appears
most clearly perhaps when he tries to work out the influence
of physical and " moral " causes on the development of the
Indians. Starting from the general assumption that " in
every part of the earth where man exists, the power of climate
operates with decisive influence upon his conditions and
character," [1] he lays it down axiomatically that the savage,
" like a plant or animal is *formed by the climate under which
he is placed.*" [2] But instead of following out this principle
to its logical conclusion he contents himself with the
conventional announcement that the inhabitants of the
temperate zones of America are more robust of body, more
active in mind, more courageous, and more attached to
liberty than those who live in the torrid region, who are
slothful, feeble in physique, and less intelligent. From
which it follows that Europeans have been most successful
in establishing their dominion in tropical America. But
even this remark required to be qualified ; for, as Robertson
points out, there is evidence to show that certain tribes in
the torrid zone (e.g. the Caribs and the peoples of Darien)
possessed courage, high spirit, and a love of independence
not inferior to the natives of more equable latitudes. Apart
from the major difficulty of accounting for the Aztec and Inca
civilizations this minor anomaly obviously troubled him, and
led him to modify considerably the general proposition with
which he started. Hence he concludes : [3] " It is not by
attending to any one single cause or principle, how powerful
and extensive soever its influence may appear, that we can
explain the actions or account for the character of men.
Even the law of climate, more universal, perhaps, in its
operation than any that affects the human species, cannot

[1] *Ibid.*, p. 398.   [2] *Ibid.*, p. 399.   [3] *Ibid.*, p. 401.

be applied, in judging of their conduct, without many exceptions."

In order to fill up the gaps in his climatic theory Robertson was led to invoke a second general principle, which he describes as "moral" or "political." According to this view the decisive influence that determines the character of peoples and their development is not the material but the social environment in which they find themselves. A savage born on the banks of the Danube differs in no respects from a savage born in the lands washed by the Mississippi ; a human being as he comes from the hand of nature is everywhere the same —his qualities and capacity for improvement are a constant quantity. In other words, the ideological development of man is independent of his geographical situation.[1] Admitted, we say ; but what light does this throw on the origin of American institutions ? And why does social environment differ so greatly throughout the world ? If climate be not the clue, where is the clue to be found ? Had Robertson been as good a philosopher as he was a historian he would have attempted to resolve the dilemma that lurks behind his incomplete and contradictory statements. As it is, he is content to establish an inconsistency. The only real value of these investigations, then, lies in the fact that they introduced rational inquiry into a subject where conjecture was rife, and thereby stimulated further research.

On the other hand, it is important to note that Robertson's realization of the value of geography as a background to history marks a great advance upon the limited views of both Voltaire and Hume. Apart from Gibbon, who fully understood the importance of such inquiries, the philosophical school of historians had a profound aversion to any interpretation savouring of materialism. Not so Robertson. Book IV of the *History of America* begins, for example, with an elaborate description of the natural conditions prevailing in the new world [2] ; the enormous extent of the *terrain* ; its mountains, rivers and lakes ; its numerous bays and estuaries suitable for commerce ; its animals, reptiles, insects, birds, and soil ; in a word, its advantages and disadvantages con-

[1] *Ibid.*, Bk. IV, p. 261. [2] *Ibid.*, pp. 240-58.

sidered as a habitat for the human race. His interest in geography, however, does not stop here. ' The question of how America was originally populated—a question dominated, at the time he wrote, by all manner of fallacious theories— took him into an investigation of Russian exploration in the Behring Sea, and led him to the conclusion that the original emigration from the Old World to America probably took place by way of Siberia and North-East Asia.[1] A flood of light was thereby thrown on American origins, and what had been a purely speculative inquiry became once again rationalized into a question of fact.

HIS THREE MASTERPIECES

Of Robertson's three great histories—the *Scotland*, the *Charles V*, and the *America*—critics have generally fixed upon the second as the most meritorious. But if the first volume, which contains the famous *View of the State of Europe*, be set aside, it would be hard to justify the eminence given to this otherwise characterless production. There is no element of greatness in the flat, insipid, and uninspiring narrative which drags its weary length through some twelve pages of print ; on the contrary, it is, for the most part, a bald chronicle of fact, ungarnished by stylistic beauties or dramatic interest of any kind. Innumerable characters make their entrances and exits ; armies march hither and thither in the interminable wars of the Valois and the Hapsburgs ; the scene shifts from Spain to Italy, or France, or Germany, or the Low Countries, or Africa, with bewildering rapidity ; great movements like the Reformation and Counter-Reformation take shape, develop, and transform the face of human society ; and behind the turmoil of the West lurks the menace of the Ottoman Turk—surely the groundwork of one of the most fascinating of historical periods ; but there is neither animation nor verisimilitude in Robertson's treatment of it. He plods his way through it all undisturbed, unimaginative, and apparently without any clear conviction of the epoch-making nature of the changes he describes. That he

[1] *Ibid.*, pp. 266-71.

was in some measure conscious of a defect in the book may
perhaps be gathered from the curious comment he makes
towards the close. " Upon reviewing the transactions of
any active epoch in the history of civilised nations," he says,[1]
" the changes which are accomplished appear wonderfully
disproportionate to the efforts which have been exerted." No
doubt : if our eyes are to be fixed on the purely political and
military detail, though even here the conclusion is scarcely
legitimate. It is certainly quite fallacious if applied to that
other aspect of the subject, the religious revolution. If this
had been given the prominence due to it, and the other transactions of the period carefully subordinated to it, there need
have been no anti-climax to the book, and in all likelihood
Robertson would have written a more attractive and convincing history. Such a supposition is, of course, tenable
only on the assumption that he was capable of infusing life
into the confessional strife—an assumption which, it must be
admitted, hardly seems warranted by the facts of the case.
His view of the Reformation, for all its superiority to Hume's,
is just as " external " as Gibbon's account of the rise of the
Christian Church. He did not realize that a great spiritual
revolution, which he frankly admits to be the most striking
since the introduction of Christianity, cannot adequately be
described by referring merely to the *actions* of the party who
supported it, or to the political causes which made success
possible. Nor is it rendered fully intelligible by enumerating
the evils of unreformed Catholicism—the corruption of the
Church, the immorality of the clergy, the immunities they
enjoyed and the wealth they possessed, the misuse of patronage by the Papacy, etc. These and other matters, such as
the influence of the printing press, the spread of a critical
spirit owing to humanist studies, and the personal character
of Luther, have, no doubt, their place in the general sum of
contributory causes ; but they are, after all, external to the
movement itself. The serious student wants to know the
position accorded to religion in society, the actual organization
and internal working of the Church during the later Middle
Ages, and the theological basis of the revolt that overthrew

[1] *Charles V*, Bk. XII, p. 506.

the old order. Robertson is silent on this deeper phase of the problem, or he is satisfied to invoke a providential " preparation of circumstances " and to leave the investigation of the purely religious aspect to the ecclesiastical historian. He will tell us nothing of the *ethos* of Protestantism, or of its significance in the development of the individual, society, or the State. His picture, in short, is mechanical, external, and without substance. Its weakness may be seen at a glance if it be studied side by side with Ranke's corresponding chapters in the *History of the Reformation in Germany*. In the one case we have formality and superficiality ; in the other a profound attempt to penetrate into the religious consciousness of the age.

If the essence of a good history be a convincing narrative the *History of Scotland* ought to be regarded as a much better work than the *Charles V*, despite the fact that it represents an earlier phase in Robertson's evolution as an historian.[1] The natural unity of the subject, the wealth of incident of an interesting character, the concentration of the interest in a few outstanding topics, the limited extent of the period covered, and the intimacy of the author with the events and movements he describes—an intimacy born of first-hand acquaintance with many of the documents—all this enabled Robertson to lavish more attention than was possible in the *Charles V* on the detailed execution of his task. Thus his character portraits are balanced with greater deliberation and insight, his epithets are more carefully selected, light and shade are more artistically distributed, and the writing is more animated.[2] Finally the descriptive passages are held in strict subordination to the development of the main theme. The consequence is that the attention of the reader is retained without effort from start to finish. Of the substance of the book it is not possible to speak in the same enthusiastic terms, because, like most historical writings, it has been overlaid by subsequent research. Nevertheless,

[1] In the great staple of all historical excellence, the narrative, it has certainly never been surpassed."—Brougham : *Lives*, etc., p. 280.

[2] Cf. his characterization of Charles V. and Francis I. (Vol. I, p. 103) ; also Beaton and Arran (*ibid.*, pp. 108-9) : and Mary Stuart (*ibid.*, I, p. 242 ; and II, p. 108).

even to-day much may be gained from its pages by the student in search of the broad features of the period. He will gain not only a vivid idea of the great events, but also a critical insight into the characters of the chief actors and the shifting motives which determined the course of the action ; he will find that at every point in the story Robertson rises superior to the facts, and subjects them boldly to the discriminating power of his own judgment. Above all, he will realize that there is no one, prince or subject, Protestant or Catholic, partisan of Mary Stuart or opponent, whose actions throughout the drama are consistently heroic and above suspicion. Robertson's deep-rooted historical scepticism is proof against the seduction of hero worship.

There can be little doubt, however, that the *History of America* represents the most massive and mature of Robertson's labours in the field of history. From whatever angle it be approached—whether as a stirring tale of " romantic valour struggling with incredible difficulties," or as a study of the growth and decay of a great experiment in Empire, it is one of the most striking monuments of the new historiography in Britain. Apart from the now obsolete sections dealing with aboriginal society prior to the Spanish invasion, the substance of the history is surprisingly good. Like the *History of Scotland*, it has the advantage of being concerned with a naturally interesting period, and with episodes that rank among the most impressive and best known in the history of the world. It is full of dramatic and inspiring contrasts, there are no involved or conflicting issues to confuse the steady unrolling of the theme, and the whole story is told with a broad humanity highly creditable to the author. The narrative excellences of the parts dealing with Columbus, Cortez, and Pizarro would be hard to beat : they are good literature as well as good history. But the most illuminating passages are those in which he inquires into the organization and structure of the Spanish Imperial Government, the treatment of the natives, the Spanish colonial system, and the subsequent modifications introduced between the sixteenth and eighteenth centuries—subjects on which public opinion was entirely wrong, or misinformed, in Robertson's day.

GIBBON

IT was customary in the eighteenth century for admiring contemporaries to allude to the author of the *Decline and Fall* as " the Gibbon "—*Le Gibbon* ; he had become, even in his own day, something of an institution in the literary world. But posterity has done far more for his name than those who hung upon his words and lionized him in the flesh. By common consent he has taken his place among the Olympians ; and no one who lays claim to a modicum of culture would now dare to confess unfamiliarity with his work ; it would be almost tantamount to confessing ignorance of Shakespeare or Magna Charta. Long before the ordinary reader summons up courage to " take him down " from the shelf, the old necromancer has cast his spell, and created the atmosphere most favourable to the performance of his wonders ; and those who by negligence, or through lack of opportunity, fail to get any further than a purely external acquaintance inflict a kind of penance on themselves by talking humbly of what they have missed. Possibly even this is an act of worship ; for, if we may believe Bagehot,[1] " the best way to reverence Gibbon " is not to come to close quarters with him at all, but to treat him as a " Yarrow unvisited," to contemplate him at a distance, and to picture what is in store for us when we grapple with his wonderful pages. What a course of events, what a muster-roll of names, what a steady, solemn sound !

It is, indeed, not advisable lightly to enter upon a study of Gibbon ; nor is it good to come to him at too early an age. He is preeminently the historian of ripe years, of men of leisure, of disillusioned spectators of life's tragi-comedy, who are prepared not to boggle over cynicism, or strain at " the immortal affectation of his unique style." To the young reader in search of the concrete facts of history he presents a

[1] Literary Studies, I, pp. 231-2.

peculiar problem—the problem, namely, of discriminating between the author and his work ; or, as it might be phrased, the problem of elucidating the information wrapped up in the most difficult and involved of literary envelopes. The untrained mind finds this a baffling and somewhat repulsive task, because Gibbon will not say the plain truth in a plain way, exactly as he perceives it. He must perforce pass it through a series of mysterious and complex processes, which polish, refine, and enrich, until eventually it emerges bedecked and bejewelled and splendid beyond recognition. But to those who are in a mind to read the *Decline and Fall* as it was intended to be read—with intentness and deliberation, and with a due regard for the play of the author's wit— there is no more fascinating document in the world. In spite of its great length, and the imposing erudition which sometimes breaks through the crust and disconcerts the general reader, its buoyancy and animation are remarkable. The specific gravity of the style is so high that it seems capable of floating anything, from the interminable Persian and Byzantine wars to the abstruse theological disputes of the Early Church and the technicalities of Justinian's legal reforms.

It is not surprising that critics, particularly literary critics, find it necessary to speak in parables when they attempt to describe Gibbon's effect on their minds ; they use the language one naturally applies to things that impress the imagination and partially elude the grasp—the language of hyperbole. Sainte-Beuve,[1] for example, compares the *Decline and Fall* to a great rear-guard action, conducted with masterly skill in the face of hostile swarms : a glorious retreat, carried out without fire or impetousity : nothing but excellent order, tactics, and deployments. To Bagehot,[2] it is like the march of a Roman legion through a troubled country, uphill and downhill, through marsh and forest, through Goth and Parthian, a well-defined array pressing to its goal, the very emblem of civilization itself. Harrison,[3] again, is reminded of a Roman triumph—some Cæsar returning from his conquests in the

---

[1] *Causeries du Lundi*, VIII, p. 456.
[2] *Literary Studies*, I, p. 226.
[3] " The Centenary of Gibbon " (*Memories and Thoughts*).

East, accompanied by all the pomp and circumstance of war : races of all colours and costumes, trophies of barbarous peoples, strange beasts, and the spoil of cities. Well might Gibbon exclaim [1] : " The captain of the Hampshire grenadiers has not been useless to the Roman Empire." Nothing would have pleased him better than to hear his book praised in terms of military imagery. But the panegyrics of posterity are not all cast in military phraseology. The ingenuity of critics has hit upon equally expressive and effective epithets drawn from civilian sources. Thus the *Decline and Fall* is said to resemble a grand *levée*, reminiscent of the days of powder and periwigs, where every one is in livery and everything is done in minuet time ; where men speak and act as they might have done at the Court of Louis XVI.[2] Or, it is compared to a splendid piece of Gothic architecture, in which the boundless range, the infinite variety, and the incongruous gorgeousness of its separate parts are all subordinated by the genius of the architect to one main and predominant theme.[3] Finally, it is said to recall the nautical scene of successive waves swelling in from the deep, and breaking with irresistible and destructive violence against some tottering fabric of man's creation.[4] In short, there is no end to the creative imagery of minds that have been touched to fine issues by the perusal of Gibbon ; nor does custom appear to " stale " his " infinite variety " to those who read him for the second, third, or even the tenth time. He is like some lofty mountain range that seems to shift and change under varying lights, and according to the angle from which it is viewed.

It is now universally admitted, however, that Gibbon's immortality is not the outcome of mere literary technique. He himself built his hopes primarily on the historical truth embodied in his book. " Diligence and accuracy," he remarked,[5] " are the only merits which an historical writer may ascribe to himself. . . . I may therefore be allowed to

[1] *Autobiography*, p. 138.
[2] Bagehot, *op. cit.*, p. 226.
[3] Milman : Preface to *Decline and Fall*.
[4] *Ibid*.
[5] *Advertisement to Notes* (First Quarto Edition).

say that I have carefully examined all the original materials that could illustrate the subject which I have undertaken to treat." Subsequent investigations and criticism, German, French, and English, have amply corroborated this claim, and Gibbon stands to-day as one of the best examples of the triumph of scholarship. Dean Milman avowed [1] that he had " the highest admiration for his general accuracy "—a verdict which Guizot also passed ; and the latest and perhaps the best qualified of all his editors, Professor Bury, expressed himself in still more emphatic terms when he wrote,[2] " If we take into account the vast range of his work, his accuracy is *amazing*." Thus it comes about that, after more than a century of historical progress, it is still advisable for the student in search of information about world history, from Augustus to the Renaissance, to find out, in the first place, what Gibbon has to say on the subject ; for, in spite of the numerous revisions, we can never be sure that his luminous page will not cast an unexpected ray of light into some dark corner. He still remains, moreover, the best guide to the main trend of human history between ancient and modern times ; and in some subjects, such as the Crusades, Moham-medanism, and the " riding monarchies of Asia," it is safe to assume that the imprint of his genius will never be effaced. This does not mean that he is invariably correct, or that his judgments are complete ; no historian can achieve finality either in his knowledge of the facts or in his judgments about them while records still remain to be explored and assimilated. But until the work of revision has issued in another synthetic history, equally illuminating, interesting, and artistic, Gib-bon's book will hold its place as the best of travelling com-panions for the period he covers.

HIS APPROACH TO THE HISTORY OF ROME

Voltaire and Hume approached the study of history com-paratively late in life, or, at all events, after their minds had reached maturity. Gibbon, on the other hand, is an instance of the happy individual who discovers his special aptitude

---

[1] *Op. cit.*, p. xli.   [2] Preface to *Decline and Fall* (1900).

in childhood. " Without engaging in a metaphysical or
rather verbal dispute," he says,[1] "*I know*, by experience,
that from earliest youth I aspired to the character of an
historian." Circumstances of an unusual kind, no doubt,
were largely responsible for this premature and precocious
aspiration. A sickly body, which prevented him from taking
part in boyish pastimes, and cut him off effectually from
regular instruction at school ; a kindly, intelligent aunt, who
acted as unofficial tutor and *confidante* during impressionable
years ; freedom to browse in libraries when his equals were
busy on the playing field, or struggling with Latin and Greek
grammar, or wasting their time over ephemeral literature ;
and, withal, an insatiable appetite for reading—all this tended
to make the youthful Gibbon a recluse and a bookworm as
soon as he could sit on a library chair and handle the ponderous folios and quartos of his day.[2] " As often as I was
tolerably exempt from danger and pain," he writes,[3] " reading,
free, desultory reading, was the employment and comfort of
my solitary hours." Of course, so early and unguided a
plunge into serious literature had its dangers : it might
have made Gibbon the very archetype of intellectual snobs,
or it might have overwhelmed his immature brain and per-
manently stunted his mental growth. As a matter of fact,
it opened to him wide vistas in the realm of human thought
and action which no schoolboy could gain for himself in the
ordinary course of education ; and it showed him, at the
earliest possible moment, where his chief interest lay, in
things of the spirit. He made this discovery, among others,
that his mind was of the positive type, that is, he belonged
to the class of readers who are content only with knowledge
of what is measurable and provable, who look to books to
provide them with a fund of reliable information, which can
be used with confidence. Now, to a mind of this cast history
was a veritable mine of wealth ; for it presented, in easily
assimilable form, a stream of fact, much of it significant in
the highest degree, starting from the dawn of human society,
and reaching down to the age in which he lived.

[1] *Autobiography*, p. 143. [2] *Ibid.*, pp. 29-42 passim.
[3] *Ibid.*, p. 43 ; " Where a title attracted my eye, without fear or awe I
snatched the volume from the shelf."—*Ibid.*, p. 39.

Before the age of fifteen, therefore, Gibbon had made his choice: his "indiscriminate appetite" had "subsided in the historic line."[1] He became immersed in the dust of old folios with as much eagerness as the average youth of to-day buries himself in tales of adventure and romance. "All that I could find," he relates,[2] "were greedily devoured from Littlebury's lame Herodotus and Spelman's valuable Xenophon, to the pompous folios of Gordon's *Tacitus* and a ragged *Procopius* of the beginning of last century. . . . From the ancient I leaped to the modern world: many crude lumps of Speed, Rapin, Mezeray, Davila, Machiavelli, Father Paul, Bower, etc., I devoured like so many novels; and I swallowed with the same voracious appetite the descriptions of India, and China, of Mexico and Peru. . . . In the summer of 1751, I accompanied my father on a visit to Mr. Hoare's, in Wiltshire; but I was less delighted with the beauties of Stourhead, than with discovering in the library a common book, the Continuation of Eachard's *Roman History*, which is indeed executed with more skill and taste than the previous work. To me the reigns of the successors of Constantine were absolutely new; and I was immersed in the passage of the Goths over the Danube, when the summons of the dinner bell reluctantly dragged me from my intellectual feast. This transient glance served rather to irritate than to appease my curiosity; and as soon as I returned to Bath I procured the second and third volumes of Howell's *History of the World*, which exhibit the Byzantine period on a larger scale. Mahomet and his Saracens soon fixed my attention; and some instinct of criticism directed me to the genuine sources. Simon Ockley, an original in every sense, first opened my eyes; and I was led from one book to another, till I had ranged round the circle of Oriental history. Before I was sixteen, I had exhausted all that could be learned in English of the Arabs and Persians, the Tartars and Turks; and the same ardour urged me to guess at the French of D'Herbelot and to construe the barbarous Latin of Pocock's *Abulfaragius*."

The congestion likely to be produced by so extensive

[1] *Ibid.*, p. 43.　　　　　　　　　　　　　　　　[2] *Ibid.*, p. 44.

reading was, to a certain extent, prevented by the use of
maps and tables, which " darted a ray of light into the
undigested chaos " ; and by the help of such aids Gibbon
was able to " distinguish the connexion of events," and to
engrave on his mind " the multitude of names and dates in
a clear and indelible series."[1] Small wonder he arrived at
Oxford (*aetas* sixteen) " with a stock of erudition that might
have puzzled a doctor, and a degree of ignorance of which a
schoolboy would have been ashamed."

In these days of highly organized research we make great
play with the blessed word " systematic." All who undertake original investigations are encouraged and instructed
to pursue their studies along rigorous and scientific lines,
leaving out nothing that is vital, but carefully limiting and
defining the goal towards which they work. Limitation and
definition, in fact, are the very essence of the business ; and
desultoriness in reading is classed with irrelevancy as the
bane of research. All this is, no doubt, excellent in theory
and practice when applied to an age like ours, of rapid book
production, and bewilderingly rich collections of records ; but
it stands in strong contrast with the leisurely methods
pursued by a writer like Gibbon. In a striking passage,
dated 1761,[2] he lays down what is practically a reversal of
the general principles now inculcated. " We must be careful," he remarks, " *not to make the order of our thoughts sub-
servient to that of our subjects ; this would be to sacrifice the
principal to the accessory.* The use of our reading is to aid us
in thinking. The perusal of a particular work gives birth,
perhaps, to ideas unconnected with the subject of which it
treats. I wish to pursue these ideas ; they withdraw me
from my proposed plan of reading, and throw me into a new
track, and from thence, perhaps, into a second, and a third.
At length I begin to perceive whither my researches tend," etc.
In other words, it is more important, in Gibbon's opinion, to
follow the bent of one's genius than to define the character
and scope of one's investigations. The way may be long, the
risks infinite, and the end problematical ; but if success
does come, if the book is eventually produced—it will be

---

[1] *Ibid.*, p. 45. [2] *Miscellaneous Works*, II, p. 2.

representative of the author's mind, in a way in which the book which is the result of mechanical devices, however scientifically applied, can never be. But the interest attaching to the quotation just cited is not its applicability to historical research in general ; it is its bearing on the career and work of Gibbon. There have been few readers so purposeful as the author of the *Decline and Fall* ; yet it is a patent fact that at no point in his preparatory studies was he perfectly clear as to where his researches would ultimately take him—not, at any rate, until his *magnum opus* was under way. It would be true, therefore, to describe the *Decline and Fall* as the culmination of a life-work, the *pensée de la jeunesse executée dans l'âge mûr*, and at the same time to regard it as the accidental outcome of a series of investigations, which, at the time they were undertaken, had no immediate bearing on the final result.

There are two turning points in Gibbon's career, viewed as a preparation for the writing of Rome's decline and downfall, beside which everything else shrinks into comparative insignificance, viz. his sojourn at Lausanne (1753–58)[1] and his visit to Rome (1764).[2] The former laid the foundations of the scholarship which Gibbon afterwards used with telling effect, and the latter revealed to him the direction in which his previous studies were irresistibly driving him ; in a word, it precipitated the decision to become the historian of Rome.

The residence at Lausanne was the result of a singular series of events and requires a word of explanation. After his irregular youthful education Gibbon was enrolled as a gentleman commoner at Magdalen College, Oxford, in 1752. The step was probably unwise ; in any case, the only thing he did there was to dodge his proper work as a undergraduate —no difficult matter at a time when " the monks of Oxford " were sunk in " port and prejudice," and the University was at a very low ebb as a teaching institution—and to continue his practice of desultory reading.[3] By accident he became

---

[1] *Autobiography*, pp. 83-110.
[2] *Ibid.*, pp. 163-4 and 167.
[3] *Ibid.*, pp. 57-8 : " The fellows or monks of my time were decent easy men, who supinely enjoyed the gifts of the founder ; their days were filled by a series of uniform employments ; the chapel and the hall, the coffee-

interested in the controversy raging round the *Free Inquiry* of Dr. Conyers Middleton, a book which, by its slashing attack on the supposed miraculous powers of the Church in the third, fourth, and fifth centuries, had created great excitement in both Catholic and Protestant circles.[1] Gibbon not only read this book : he apparently read all the correspondence it occasioned, and then plunging deeper and deeper into Catholic apologetics, finished appropriately with Bossuet, the prince of controversialists. " I surely fell," he comments,[2] " by a noble hand." The result was that he not only acknowledged himself convinced, *by the weight of historical evidence*, of the validity of the Catholic position, but recanted his Protestantism and was privately received into the Church of Rome on June 8, 1753.[3]

From the moment this became known it was obvious that Gibbon's career at Oxford was ended, and indeed his position in England was precarious ; for it was still a treasonable offence to be reconciled to Rome.[4] The only thing to do, in the circumstances, was to despatch the culprit abroad ; and this his father promptly did, choosing as tutor a certain M. Pavilliard, Protestant pastor at Lausanne.[5] Here, in the house of his new teacher, Gibbon lived for the next five years, and they proved to be the most important five years in his life. " Whatever may have been the fruits of my education," he writes,[6] " they must be ascribed to the fortunate banishment which placed me at Lausanne." Rapidly he was weaned by the tact and genius of M. Pavilliard, and by debates with the able clergy of the *pays du Vaud*, from " the errors of the church of Rome " ; and almost exactly eighteen months after his first conversion he was re-converted, receiving the sacrament according to the Protestant rite on Christmas day, 1754.[7]

We are not to suppose, however, that Gibbon now returned,

---

house and the common room, till they retired, weary and well satisfied, to a long slumber. . . . Their conversation stagnated in a round o. college business, Tory politics, personal anecdotes, and private scandal."
" The sum of my improvements in the university of Oxford is confined to three or four Latin plays."—*Ibid.*, p. 60.

[1] *Ibid.*, pp. 67-8.   [2] *Ibid.*, p. 70.   [3] *Ibid.*, p. 72
[4] *Ibid.*, p. 73.   [5] *Ibid.*, pp. 82-3.   [6] *Ibid.*, p. 108.
[7] *Ibid.*, p. 90.

a penitent, to the bosom of dogmatic Protestantism : far
from it. The seductive, sceptical, atmosphere of French
literature, which he appears to have imbibed while at
Lausanne, the expansion of his mind through contact with an
alien civilization, together with the progress he made in
philosophical studies, greatly blunted his early appetite for
theology, and produced in his mind a state of suspended
animation so far as religious inquiry was concerned. To
all intents and purposes he became a follower of the
comfortable, generalized creed of Deism, the home of
the disillusioned, who sought an escape from theological
dogma without surrendering their belief in the moral life.
But the real import of Gibbon's stay in Switzerland rests
much more upon the hard course of study he undertook in
Latin literature than upon the curious mental adjustments to
which allusion has just been made. His efforts in this direction were indeed remarkable. Apart from his favourite
authors of the Augustan Age he appears to have read practically everything worth reading " from Plautus and Sallust
to the decline of the language and empire of Rome." And
this extensive reading was punctuated with critical notes,
essays, and correspondence on disputed points with learned
commentators in Paris, Zurich, and Göttingen.[1] Probably,
if he had been able to overcome the necessary drudgery he
would have made himself equally proficient at Greek—a
language which, he frankly confesses, he never really
mastered.[2] But, even as it was, when he returned to England in 1758 he could boast himself an accomplished Latin
scholar and a fluent writer in French. The foundations of
his future researches were securely laid.

The second turning point was reached some six years
later. The interval, though marked by the publication of the
juvenile *Essai sur l'Étude de la Littérature* [3]—a tribute to
the value of his classical studies, and by a good deal of cogita-
tion on possible subjects for the great historical work that

[1] *Ibid.*, pp. 90-3.
[2] *Ibid.*, p. 95 : " My ardour, destitute of aid and emulation, was gradually
cooled, and, from the barren task of searching words in a lexicon, I withdrew
to the free and familiar conversation of Virgil and Tacitus."
[3] *Ibid.*, pp. 123-34.

would, in due course, immortalize his name[1]—was largely
a barren period in his life. To the inevitable distractions
of society at Buriton, his father's residence, were added the
further distractions of a war with France ; and Gibbon
" with Horace in his knapsack," captained for two years a
company of Hampshire Volunteers.[2] It was not, in fact,
until the restoration of peace between England and France,
in 1763, that a resumption of serious study became possible.
And once, again, by a curious coincidence, the scene of this
second bout of hard work was Lausanne. Early in the year,
as soon as he could divest himself of the King's commission,
he persuaded his father to send him on a continental tour—
" to enjoy," as he said,[3] " the society of a polished and amiable
people, in whose favour I was strongly prejudiced." But
if Paris was the immediate goal he had in view, Italy was
the magnet that drew him. After a round of the *salons*,[4]
where he was well received, as the author of the *Essai*, and a
visit to the " various treasures of art, of learning, and of
luxury,"[5] he made his way to his old haunts by the " Leman
lake " ; and, in congenial surroundings, began to prepare
himself for a memorable year in Italy. Surely there never
was a more amazing prelude to a holiday ! But we must let
him tell his own tale. " I diligently read," he writes,[6]
" almost always with my pen in my hand, the elaborate
treatises of Nardini, Donatus, etc., which fill the fourth
volume of the Roman antiquities of Grævius. I next undertook and finished the *Italia Antiqua* of Cluverius, a learned
native of Prussia, who had measured, on foot, every spot,
and has compiled and digested every passage of the ancient
authors. These passages in Greek or Latin authors I perused
in the text of Cluverius, in two folio volumes ; but I separately
read the descriptions of Italy by Strabo, Pliny, and Pom-
ponius Mela, the Catalogues of the Epic poets, the Itineraries

[1] *Ibid.*, pp. 143-7 : E.g. Charles VIII, the Crusade of Richard I, the Barons'
War, the Black Prince, Henry V and the Emperor Titus, Sir Philip Sidney,
the Marquis of Montrose, Sir Walter Raleigh, the History of Swiss Liberty,
Florence under the De Medicis.
[2] *Ibid.*, p. 142 : " On every march, in every journey, Horace was always
in my pocket, and often in my hand."
[3] *Ibid.*, p. 150.   [4] *Ibid.*, pp. 152-3.   [5] *Ibid.*, p. 149.
[6] *Ibid.*, pp. 151-9.

of Wesseling's Antoninus, and the coasting voyage of Rutilius Numatianus, and I studied two kindred subjects in the *Mésures Itinéraires* of D'Anville, and the copious work of Bergier, *Histoire des Grands Chemins de l'Empire Romain*. From these materials I formed a table of roads and distances reduced to our English measure ; filled a folio common-place book with my collections and remarks on the geography of Italy ; and inserted in my journal many long and learned notes on the *insulæ* and populousness of Rome, the social war, the passage of the Alps by Hannibal, etc. After glancing my eye over Addison's agreeable dialogues, I seriously read the great work of Ezechiel Spanheim, *De Præstantia et Usu Numismatum*, and applied with him the medals of the kings and emperors, the families and colonies, to the illustration of the ancient history. And thus was I armed for my Italian journey."[1]

Excellent as this summary is it gives but a poor idea of the extent of Gibbon's labours, and none at all of the ambitious designs now taking shape in his head. The ninety-two folio pages he refers to were to have been the nucleus of an epoch-making work on the geography of ancient Italy which would supersede Cluverius. In the Journal, under the date December 7, 1763, he entered a lengthy note describing the plan he proposed to follow.[2] Briefly, his idea was to begin with Romulus and to trace the genesis and growth of the nation down to Augustus. By this " luminous and natural " arrangement the prospective reader would be in a position to follow the progress of the Roman arms, and Livy's history, as well as gain a sound knowledge of Italian geography. " A work of this kind," he comments, " well executed, would be favourably received by the public. It would enrich a bookseller, pass through ten editions and become a classical book with students, colleges, travellers, and even men of letters."

The scheme, it need hardly be said, was never realized ; for the simple reason that it was overlaid and obliterated, like all Gibbon's earlier schemes, by subsequent and more ambitious conceptions. Its importance lies in the fact that

---

[1] The record of his reading is much more fully detailed in the *Miscellaneous Works*, II, pp. 94-303.   [2] *Ibid.*, p. 247.

it indicates a first attempt to focus his studies on a theme
connected with Roman history ; it was, in effect, the first
dim groping towards his true vocation as a scholar. The
decisive event that shattered it was the visit to Rome in
October, 1764. " It was at Rome," he tells us,[1] in a much-
quoted passage of the *Autobiography*, " as I sat musing
amidst the ruins of the Capitol, while the bare-footed friars
were singing vespers in the Temple of Jupiter, that the idea
of writing the decline and fall of the city first entered my
mind." Here, at last, then, we reach the moment of illumination in the life of Gibbon, the psychological crisis, when, by
a flash of inspiration, he grasped the real drift of his studies.[2]
He might subsequently modify the idea now germinating in
his brain, he might expand it almost out of recognition by
substituting for " city " " empire," but he could no longer
escape the destiny that marked him down as the historian
of Rome.

Several years were still to elapse, however, before Gibbon
could transmute the vision into the cold reality of laborious
research. For a time he contemplated it from a distance,
took refuge in an abortive attempt to write the history of
Swiss liberty,[3] wrote articles for an equally abortive journal
entitled *Mémories Littéraires de la Grande Bretagne*, in col-
laboration with his Swiss friend Deyverdun ;[4] and followed
this up by " breaking a lance against the giant's shield "
of Warburton over the interpretation of Book VI of the
Æneid.[5] But by 1768 the spell was upon him ; he " began
gradually to advance from the wish to the hope, from the
hope to the design, from the design to the execution."[6]

---

[1] Page 167.
[2] " Et de temps en temps, dans la continuité de sa grave Histoire, on
croira entendre revenir comme par contraste ce chant de vêpres du premier
jour, cette impression dénigrante qu'il ramènera à la sourdine."—Sainte-
Beuve, *op. cit.*, p. 453.
[3] *Ibid.*, pp. 171-2.
[4] *Ibid.*, p. 173.
[5] *Ibid.*, pp. 177-80.
[6] *Ibid.*, p. 181 : " I insensibly plunged," he continues, " into the ocean
of Augustan history ; and in the descending series I investigated, with my
pen almost always in my hand, the original records, both Greek and Latin,
from Dion Cassius to Ammianus Marcellinus, from the reign of Trajan to the
last age of the Western Cæsars. The subsidiary rays of medals and inscrip-
tions, of geography and chronology, were thrown on their proper objects,

Five years later the composition of Volume I of the *Decline
and Fall of the Roman Empire* was begun.

HIS METHOD

Gibbon, we have said, was marked out by nature for the
rôle of historian. He had no battle to wage against a super-
abundant imagination and subjectivity, which is the lot of
many a worker in the historical field. His positive and
methodical mind was untiring in its pursuit of the real and
tangible, and his reading was consistently devoted to the
supreme task of increasing his stock of useful information.
"Nothing ran through his mind," writes a contemporary;[1]
"every subject worthy of attention was sifted, examined,
and dissected. . . . It was impossible for him to be super-
ficial." He had, in fact, a scholar's mania for collecting
relevent detail of all kinds, and an equally remarkable
capacity for digesting, recording, and assimilating it. A
day spent without some calculable gain to be entered in his
Journal, or written out at greater length in a commonplace
book, was a day misspent, and therefore to be regretted.
The use of pen and paper was, indeed, a second nature to him.
At one time we find him commenting upon the height of
Chimborazo, or noting the temperature of molten lava, or
reading about the hatching of eggs, the habits of bees and
fishes, the plants of Switzerland, or the climate of Siberia
and Iceland.[2] At another time, when the mood is upon him,
he pursues elaborate investigations into ancient weights and
measures,[3] balances rival systems of chronology,[4] delves into
the antiquities of Rome,[5] the history of the Medes [6] and the
Swiss,[7] the Feudal System,[8] or the claim of Charles VIII to

and I applied the collections of Tillemont, whose inimitable accuracy almost
assumes the character of genius, to fix and arrange within my reach the loose
and scattered atoms of historical information. Through the darkness of
the Middle Ages, I explored my way in the Annals and Antiquities of Italy of
the learned Muratori . . . till I almost grasped the ruins of Rome in the
fourteenth century," etc.

[1] Rev. Norton Nicholls ; *vide Miscellaneous Works*, III, pp. 677-8.
[2] *Miscellaneous Works*, II, passim.   [3] *Ibid.*, III, p. 442.
[4] *Ibid.*, p. 61.   [5] *Ibid.*, p. 239, and II, pp. 321-402.
[6] *Ibid.*, III, p. 1.   [7] *Ibid.*, III, p. 98.   [8] *Ibid.*, III, p. 83.

the crown of Naples.[1] Within the limits set by his passion
for the concrete, his range of interests was boundless.

Now, while this acquisitive turn of mind is not peculiar
to the historian, it is, nevertheless, common to all investigators, and is the basis of scientific work in every department
of intellectual activity. All great books must be, in one
aspect at least, repositories of factual knowledge, records
of careful observation. And if we approach Gibbon's *History*
from this point of view it will be seen to be one of the most
impressive books ever written. What an array of statistics
it contains, what a repertory of exact information it is, what
a triumph of accumulation ! Distances between places, the
situation of towns, the courses followed by rivers—their
length, depth, and speed—the detail of a Persian banquet,
a Gothic cathedral, or a Roman amphitheatre, the intricacies
of a theological dispute or the Roman law, the composition
of Greek fire, or the origin of silk manufacture in Europe—
there is no topic, connected with his theme even remotely,
which he did not master and write about with authority.
The *Decline and Fall*, in fact, is a book without fringes ;
it has no penumbra, so to speak, where the author's vision
fades away into the dim realm of half lights and conjecture :
the whole work stands out as sharply and clearly as a rock
crystal.

But diligence and precision in mastering detail is by no
means the most important part of Gibbon's equipment as a
historian. He was too attached to the philosophical school
of his day to lay more than a qualified stress on purely factual
knowledge ; and the *compilateur grossier*, who made facts
the be-all and end-all of his professional existence, only
excited his ridicule. The office of historian, he once remarked[2]
is as honourable as that of a mere compiler is contemptible.
His bias in this matter is as great as Voltaire's, and no whit
less bluntly expressed. From the candidate for historical
honours he demanded sweep of vision, justness of perception,
and, above all, the ability to detect the causal relationship
between events.[3] "History," he comments,[4] "is for the

[1] *Ibid.*, II, p. 6.
[2] *Ibid.*, II, p. 23, and *Essai sur L'Étude de la Littérature*, lii.
[3] *Essai*, xliv-lv.   [4] *Ibid.*, xlviii.

philosophic mind (*esprit philosophique*) what gaming was to
the Marquis de Dangeau. He saw in it a system, connections
a sequence, while others discerned only the caprices of
fortune." True, he would say, all facts are potentially
valuable : the historian may with advantage copy the
botanist, who continues to study the properties of plants
whether they have any immediate use in medicine or not ;[1]
but the distinguishing mark by which we know him is his
capacity for searching out the dominating facts which, so to
speak, set the springs in motion (*qui en ont fait mouvoir les
ressorts*).[2] Thus history, in Gibbon's eyes, is much more
than a correct record of fact : it is an organized sequence
of cause and effect, justly proportioned.[3] Design forms its
very warp and woof.

It must not be supposed, however, that when Gibbon
invokes the *esprit philosophique* in history he means precisely
the same thing as Voltaire or Hume understood by it. He
would not have subscribed, for example, to the celebrated
maxim that history is " philosophy teaching by examples " ;
on the contrary, he would have repudiated, most emphatically,
any attempt to subordinate historical truth to philosophical
theory.[4] The fact is, Gibbon was not a philosopher in the
strict sense of the word. He has nothing to say of the ultimate
meaning of the events he describes, nor is there any
" schematic tendency " traceable in his history comparable
to that which dominates the pages of his thorough-paced
contemporaries. He may, it is true, moralize occasionally
over the tragi-comedy of the world spectacle as it transacts
itself before his eyes ; he may point a scornful finger at the
follies and foibles of mankind, saint and sinner alike ; he

---

[1] *Ibid.*, liii : " Imitons les botanistes. Toutes les plantes ne sont pas
utiles dans la médicine, cependant ils ne cessent d'en découvrir de nouvelles."
[2] *Ibid*, xlix : " Parmi la multitude des faits, il y en a, et c'est le grand
nombre, qui ne procurent rien au-dèla de leur propre existence. . . . Ceux
qui dominent dans le système général, qui y sont liés intimément, et qui en
ont fait mouvoir les ressorts, sont fort rares, et il est plus rare encore de trouver,
des esprits qui sachent les entrevoir dans la vaste cahos des événements,
et les en tirer purs et sans melanges."
[3] *Ibid* : " À ceux qui ont plus de jugement que d'érudition, il paraîtra peu
nécessaire d'avertir qu'on doit toujours proportionner les causes aux effets."
[4] He asserts, however, that historians should be philosophers : " Si les
philosophes ne sont pas toujours historiens, il serait du moins à souhaiter
que les historiens fussent philosophes " (*Ibid.*, lii).

may give play to his sceptical temperament, and suffuse whole chapters with a grave and sometimes pitiless irony—but all this is merely the running comment of a lively and gifted intelligence, elicited by the impact of facts on the mind. It cannot by any stretch of the imagination be called philosophy. From first to last Gibbon's main concern as a historical writer is, as it should be, to describe the past: "To render to posterity a just and perfect delineation of all that may be praised, of all that may be excused, and of all that may be censured."[1] The ultimate meaning and value of the historical *processus* in general he leaves to the reader, who will draw his own conclusions and form his own judgments.

On the whole, therefore, we are justified in assuming that when Gibbon speaks of the use of the "philosophic mind" he refers to the form rather than the matter of history. In non-technical language it was simply the faculty, possessed by the true historian and lacking in the mere compiler, for systematically integrating the details unearthed by study into a unified and orderly whole. In a passage of the *Autobiography*[2] he tells us that it was his usual practice, on acquiring a new book, first to question himself concerning the existing state of his information on the matter discussed. He was then in a position to extract the greatest benefit from its perusal. The consequence of this rigorous and salutary procedure was that he could marshal and apply the whole available stock of his knowledge at any moment to the determination of each specific point that might arise. Acquisitiveness was therefore fortified and supplemented at every turn by constructive criticism, and the raw material of reading was steadily transmuted into a connected and orderly view of the entire subject in which he happened to be interested. It helped also in the same direction that Gibbon never allowed ideas or facts to lie dormant and unfruitful in his mind or in his notebook; he kept turning them over, held stocktakings, as it were, which occupied him for days and weeks, when he would reduce his intellectual acquisitions to their capital value, in a literary form.

---

[1] *A Vindication, etc.*, (*Miscellaneous Works*, II, p. 596).
[2] Page 122.

This practice of assessing one's intellectual progress is, again, not peculiar to historians, but it is the only way by which the human mind, in continual danger of sinking under the growing burden of fact, may advance to the execution of a great design in any department of research. It shows the architectonic faculty at work, and without it no permanent contribution to knowledge can ever be made. Thus Gibbon's various essays, disquisitions, summaries, and jottings may be regarded as so many stages in his preparation for the *Decline and Fall.*

The habit of applying the knowledge he possessed, of putting it out into circulation, of exercising it, might be illustrated in different ways from the pages of the Journal. Take, for instance, the following two excerpts :

M. Guichardt (Mémoires Militaires sur les Grecs et les Romains, tom. II, p. 220) attributes the stay of Cæsar in Egypt not to Cleopatra, but to the Etesian winds, which Hirtius seems to confirm.   But this reason or pretence could only relate to a very inconsiderable part of the nine months (Appian de Bell. Civil. I, ii, p. 484) which he spent there ; since the season of the Etesian winds is over some time before the autumnal equinox (V. Plin. Hist. Natur., I, ii, c. 47) and Cæsar did not land in Egypt before the middle of August.   The proof of this depends upon an accurate survey of the then irregular Roman calendar.   I adopt the system of M. de la Nauze (V. Mémoires de la Littérature, tom. XXVI) as it appears to me far more probable than that of Archbishop Usher, etc."[1]

Or, take this devastating onslaught on a sentence of Joseph Warton :

The author of the Adventurer, No. 127 (Mr. Joseph Warton, concealed under the signature of Z) concludes his ingenious parallel of the ancients and moderns by the following remark : " That age will never again return ; when a Pericles, after walking with Plato in a portico built by Phidias, and painted by Apelles, might repair to hear a pleading of Demosthenes, or a tragedy of Sophocles."   It will never return because it never existed.

[1] *Index Expurgatorius (Miscellaneous Works*, III, pp. 555-6).

Pericles (who died in the fourth year of the LXXXIXth Olympiad, Ant. ch. 429, Dio. Sic. l. xii, 46) was confessedly the patron of Phidias, and the contemporary of Sophocles ; but he could enjoy no very great pleasure in the conversation of Plato, who was born in the same year that he himself died. (Diogenes Laertius in Platone, V. Stanley's History of Philosophy, p. 154). The error is still more extraordinary with regard to Apelles and Demosthenes since both the painter and the orator survived Alexander the Great, whose death is above a century posterior to that of Pericles (in 323) etc." [1]

Scholarship, it has been wisely said, must always be judged in relation to its opportunities. Had Gibbon been born a century later, and confronted with the vast stores of information which scholars have piled up since his day, it is safe to assume that the *Decline and Fall* would never have been written ; the task of assimilation over so wide a field has long ago become too great for one man to accomplish, however gifted. If, in addition, he had become immersed in palæography, diplomatic, *Quellenkritik*, and the other subsidiary studies now recognized to be part and parcel of the historian's training, the chances are that he might not have risen even to the conception of a sustained organic work. At any rate, a " palæographical " Gibbon is virtually inconceivable. He was what he was by dint of the fact that he did not consume his time in the labours to which Mabillon, Tillemont, and the antiquarian school which preceded him dedicated their lives. Instinctively he felt that his special genius lay in appreciating and working up into literary form what the researchers in the mine brought to the surface, not in spelling out laboriously the sense of ancient manuscripts. The *inédit*, in short, had no attractions for him.[2] Consequently, when he claimed that it was his habit " to examine all the original materials that could

---

[1] *Ibid.*, p. 565.
[2] Nevertheless Gibbon lent his support to a movement for printing a *corpus* of English mediaeval records. In an " Address " (*Miscell. Works*, II, p. 707 *et seq.*) he pleads for a collection of *Scriptores Rerum Anglicarum*, after the manner of Muratori, Langebek, and the great German and French repositories. Incidentally, he has a word of praise for all the patient researchers, who, up to his own time, had enriched the national store of material—Polydore Virgil, Camden, Selden, Wheeler, Gibson, Watts, Dugdale, Warton, Wilkins, Twysden, Gale, and Thomas Hearne.

illustrate the subject " he referred only to those accessible in print. This fortunate limitation, then, was the condition of his life-work.

On the other hand, while it is important to make certain reservations when judging of Gibbon's work, something must be said concerning the kind of deficiency from which the *Decline and Fall* suffers.[1] In the first place, the most striking change that has come over historical method since it was written is the increased attention paid to the ascertainment of correct *data* ; the investigation of sources and their evaluation has been elevated to the level of a science in itself. The question now is, not what such and such an authority says, but on what ground and with what validity he says it. Under the continuous scrutiny of this newer erudition the very material out of which history is made has been changed, sometimes almost out of recognition ; authorities on whom Gibbon implicitly relied, have been rejected as more or less valueless, and statements which he received as true have been proved to be mere romance. For instance, Procopius, whose "Secret History" supplied him with the greater part of his material for the reign of Justinian, whose scandalous tales he quotes freely in his notes, has been successfully impugned as a satirist, calumniator, and party writer.[2] The same fate has befallen Al Wakidi, the authority on whom, indirectly, Gibbon constructed his enthralling chapter on Moham-medanism ; it appears that he wrote his Life of Mahomet at Bagdad, and "necessarily lent himself to the perversion of tradition in the Abbassid interest."

In the next place, it was Gibbon's habit sometimes to commit the crime of combining evidence derived from different periods in order to fill out the paucity of informa-tion available on the subject he happened to be handling— a practice now condemned as mischievous and unhistorical. A good example of the method at work may be seen in his account of the manners and customs of the Germans. In order to impart an artistic unity to the narrative he skil-fully weaves together the facts supplied by both Cæsar and

---

[1] *Vide* Bury : *Introduction to Decline and Fall* (1900), pp. xlv-lxvii.
[2] Cf. Bury : *The Later Roman Empire*, II, pp. 423-4.

Tacitus, ignoring the changes that took place during the hundred years that separated the two accounts. The result, of course, is a picture ideally satisfying to the mind, but historically misleading and fallacious. A scrappy description that reflected the actual state of the evidence would have been more satisfactory.

Finally, the progress of research, in greatly extending the available information over the entire field covered by Gibbon, has necessarily resulted in a change in the perspective. Where he passed lightly with a reference the modern historian amplifies and elaborates, sometimes to vast proportions. The change is perhaps most noticeable in regard to Byzantine history, the significance of which Gibbon altogether misconceived and under-estimated. It is now clear that from Leo the Isaurian to Basil II the account given in the *Decline and Fall* is no longer useful even as a sketch ; the theory of uniform corruption and decadence, on which it is founded, is described by Professor Bury as " one of the most untrue judgments ever uttered by a thoughtful historian."

Other points on which progress has been registered, and on which Gibbon's masterpiece is out of date, might easily be added : such as the study of topography and architecture, and the opening up of research into the antiquities of those peoples whose history impinged on the Eastern Empire— Bulgars, Roumanians, Hungarians, Russians. But sufficient has been said to indicate the directions in which Gibbon must be supplemented or controlled by the modern student ; for detailed information recourse must be had to the copious notes and appendices attached by Professor Bury to his edition of the *Decline and Fall*.

THE DECLINE AND FALL

If, as we have suggested, one ought to look for design rather than a philosophical system in Gibbon, what, it may be asked, was the design on which he constructed his history of Rome's downfall ? Or, putting it more concretely, what was the theme he proposed to exemplify in it ? Briefly, it may be said that the title itself is its own best " table of

contents." To Gibbon the history of Europe, and indeed
of the world, from Aurelius to the extinction of the Western
Empire in A.D. 476, appears in the light of a tragic catastrophe, or, as Professor Bury puts it,[1] a retrogression, which
involved in common ruin, not merely the laws, institutions,
and civilization of Rome itself, but also the security, prosperity, culture, and happiness of the most significant part of
the human race. " If," he says,[2] " a man were called to fix
the period in the history of the world, during which the
condition of the human race was most happy and prosperous,
he would, without hesitation, name that which elapsed from
the death of Domitian to the accession of Commodus."
Again and again, in the course of his *History*, Gibbon reverts
to this pristine or golden age, to measure against it, as against
an absolute standard,[3] the degeneracy of the times he is
actually describing. He accepts the organization of Rome,
and almost worships its spirit. The Roman genius for
toleration, law, and order, the complete absence of fanaticism,
the *Pax Romana* which safeguarded the world from violence
and war, the mildness of the Roman magistrate, the wisdom
of the Roman philosopher—this was conceived by Gibbon
as the normal and necessary basis of civil society in the world,
departure from which spells disaster to the body politic of
mankind. From which it follows, logically, that he cannot
write temperately, or in the language of a completely dis-
interested spectator, of that other aspect of his subject, to
which the facts he adduces ought, strictly speaking, to have
called his attention, viz. the new principle of life and energy
imparted to the world by the barbarian races, and particularly by the Christian Church. In virtue of this theme
he cannot, and will not, do justice to the growth of the papal
monarchy and the ecclesiastical organization of Europe,
which, springing from the ashes of a decadent world, became,

---

[1] Introduction to *Decline and Fall*, p. xxxviii.
[2] *Decline and Fall*, I, p. 78.
[3] E.g. " If it be possible to measure the interval between the philosophic
writings of Cicero and the sacred legend of Theodoret, between the character
of Cato and that of Simeon, we may appreciate the memorable revolution
which was accomplished in the Roman empire within a period of five hundred
years."—*Ibid.*, IV. p. 75. Cf. also the following passages : II, p. 114, 159 ;
IV, pp. 53-4 ; V. p. 93.

in the course of centuries, the nucleus of a new and ultimately more enlightened order. 'His theme was decay, and, like the artist he was, he refused to introduce a discordant note. For him, as for Hume, European history in the Middle Ages represented a " trough " in the development of humanity.

There is no doubt, of course, that this stubborn consistency of Gibbon lends great majesty, impressiveness, and pathos to his History. It enables him to marshal his facts, arrange his topics, and set his narrative marching steadily in one direction ; and this, incidentally, is the essence of a literary masterpiece, whether it be an epic, a drama, or a novel. In fact, the effect produced by the *Decline and Fall* is comparable only with that produced by literary works of the first rank ; it stimulates not only the intellect, but also the imagination, and the reader lays down the book with a reflection on the transitoriness of human greatness, the inevitability of decay, and a sense of irreparable loss.

It might be supposed that since Gibbon entitled his work *The Decline and Fall of the Roman Empire* a goodly part of it would consist in an analysis of the causes of the disaster. We should expect him to diagnose the disease or diseases from which it perished, to lay a finger on the flaw of the organism, or in some way to indicate when and how the great structure was undetermined and toppled over. A modern historian working over the same ground would certainly concentrate his attention on this aspect of the subject. But not so Gibbon. In the first place, he is descriptive rather than analytical, that is, he does not greatly concern himself with the subterranean forces at work, but dwells on what is visible, tangible, and on the surface. A great drama is presented to the reader, in which all the actors move and act according to their separate parts ; but there is no explanation of why the drama took the form it did ; no attempt to display the secret springs that set it in motion and controlled its various developments. This does not mean that the *Decline and Fall* is a book without a clue ; as we shall see presently, there are several clues embedded in the text ; but there is nothing in the shape of a sustained and reasoned analysis of the facts described, no effort to place them

" beneath the deeper sky of social evolution."[1] Gibbon was content to set the puppets in motion ; he left it to succeeding writers to penetrate behind the scenes and discover the laws which determined the course of events.   In the second place, it seems fairly clear that when he began his *History*, he had not clarified his own mind as to where he ought to lay the emphasis. The consequence is that the clues he supplies vary from time to time, and the reader is mystified as to what Gibbon really intended to convey. For example, in Chapter II[2] he attributes the calamities of the empire to the long peace and the uniform government, which reduced men's minds to the same level, extinguished the fire of genius, and weakened the military spirit.   In Chapter VII,[3] with a wider conspectus of fact under his eye, he develops this idea still further. The Romans, he says, built up a great empire by dint of their genius for war and government—virtues they acquired in the hard school of poverty. But their success dissolved them into the common mass of mankind, and confounded them with millions of servile provincials. Consequently they lost the spirit by which they had risen, became discouraged in industry, relaxed in discipline, and so feeble in war that they allowed their empire to be ravished from them by the barbarians. In short, a race of pygmies had succeeded to a race of giants. In Chapter XXVII,[4] again, he strikes a new note, and lays emphasis on luxury and the effeminacy accompanying it. This canker, he asserts, originating in courts and cities, "instilled a secret and destructive poison into the camps of the legionaries." From which it follows that the pusillanimous indolence of the army induced by luxury is the immediate cause of the empire's downfall. But in the same breath he explains that this same luxury and effeminacy were not a cause but an effect : " The mad prodigality which prevails in the confusion of a shipwreck or a siege may serve to explain the progress of luxury

[1] Leslie Stephen, *Studies of a Biographer*, I (Gibbon's *Autobiography*) : " He calmly surveys the great stream of history, its mingling currents and deluges and regurgitations, the struggles of priests and warriors and legislators, without suggesting any adequate conceptions of what is called the social dynamics implied."
[2] *Decline and Fall*, II, p. 58.   [3] *Ibid.*, pp. 193-4.
[4] *Ibid.*, III, pp. 186-7.

amidst the misfortunes and terrors of a sinking nation."
Clearly there is something wrong with the argument ; what
is a cause of something cannot, at the same time, be a result
of it : we cannot have it both ways. If luxury was a cause
of Rome's downfall, it seems impossible to describe it also
as the result of the catastrophe. In Chapter XXXV[1] he
continues his analysis, and on this occasion brings forward
a theory which he has so far completely neglected—a socio-
economic explanation. Stress is now laid on the unequal
distribution of taxation, and the distress of the population
owing to the callousness of the rich, who shuffle off their
share of public burdens on to the shoulders of those who
are least able to bear them. As a result of this, Gibbon
points out, men refused to take up the duties of citizenship,
and abhorred the name of Roman citizen, which had formerly
excited the ambition of mankind. It would appear that he
attached much more importance to this " flight from citizenship " than to the military collapse ; for, he adds, " If all
the barbarians had been annihilated in the same hour, their
total destruction would not have restored the empire of the
West." The most complete analysis, however, is reserved
for Chapter XXXVIII,[2] under the title " General Observations on the Fall of the Roman Empire in the West."
Having now viewed the entire course of events in their
sequence, he is convinced that the catastrophe was due to the
operation of law rather than to a series of accidents.   " The
decline of Rome," he remarks, " was the *natural and inevitable
effect of immoderate greatness*.   Prosperity ripened the principle
of decay : the causes of destruction multiplied with the
extent of the conquest ; and as soon as time or accident had
removed the artificial supports, the stupendous fabric *yielded
to the pressure of its own weight* : and instead of inquiring
why the Roman empire was destroyed, we should rather be
surprised that it subsisted so long."

These last words are pregnant with suggestiveness. To
readers of Montesquieu they seem to be almost an echo of
the thesis so brilliantly developed in the *Grandeur et Decadence
des Romains*, a work with which Gibbon was well acquainted.

---

[1] *Ibid.*, III, p. 480.   [2] *Ibid.*, IV, pp. 160-4.

" Here is the history of the Romans in a nutshell," wrote Montesquieu.[1] " They conquered all people by their maxims ; but when they achieved this, *their republic could not subsist : it was necessary to change the government* ; and maxims contrary to the former, employed in this new government, were the cause of their downfall." It will be observed, however, that Gibbon really commits himself to a much bolder assertion than that Rome's collapse was due to her expansion. In the sentence " Prosperity ripened the principle of decay," he makes use of a biological analogy, and would appear to imply that the seeds of decay, already implicit in the organism of the Roman State, required only the sun of prosperity to render them active and destructive. Did he mean to suggest that there is something in the life of States akin to the biological phenomenon of senescence in the life of the physical organism ? The idea bears on its face so obvious a mark of modernity that we might be inclined to dismiss it as improbable in the eighteenth century if Walter Moyle, the antiquary, had not ventilated it in still more explicit terms some fifty years before Gibbon wrote.[2] Just in the same way, said Moyle, as physical bodies carry in their organization the principles of their dissolution, so also artificial bodies like States and Republics have in their constitution flaws and vices which merely await the corruption of the times in order to develop and produce their destruction. Whether Gibbon borrowed the idea from this source, which is not unlikely, or was himself the originator of it, it is certainly remarkable that he should have hit upon the most fascinating and seductive of all speculative theories concerning the fate of Rome. If Lord Balfour is right in his surmise, it is possible that biology may yet have a decisive word to utter on the subject. " When through an ancient and still powerful State," he remarks,[3] " there spreads a mood of deep-discouragement,

[1] Chap. XVIII : " Ce n'est pas la fortune qui domine le monde ; on peut le demander aux Romains, qui eurent une suite continuelle de prospérités quand ils se gouvernèrent sur un certain plan, et une suite non interrompue de revers quand ils se conduisirent sur un autre. Il y a des causes générales, soit morales, soit physiques, qui agissent dans chaque monarchie, l'élèvent, la maintiennent, ou la précipitent," etc.

[2] *Essay on the Constitution of the Roman Government.*

[3] *Decadence* (Henry Sidgwick Memorial Lecture, 1908), p. 34.

when the reaction against recurring ills grows feebler and the ship rises less buoyantly to each succeeding wave, when learning languishes, enterprise slackens, and vigour ebbs away, then, as I think, there is present some process of social degeneration, which we must perforce recognize, and which, pending a satisfactory analysis, may conveniently be distinguished by the name of decadence."

From the historical standpoint, however, all such analogies, suggestive as they may be to the philosophic mind, are suspect and dangerous ; and for the simple reason that history is primarily concerned with specific causes. The theory of natural and inevitable decline, voiced in different ways by Moyle, Montesquieu, and Gibbon, may represent the high-water mark of eighteenth century speculation on Rome's downfall ; but it is of less value to the historical inquirer than the individual causes which Gibbon enumerates ; these at all events can be checked, controverted, or supplemented, as the case may be : not so the former, which has no basis in known facts and belongs to a totally different department of inquiry. The causes which Gibbon enumerates may be merely accompaniments, or symptoms, of deeper seated maladies in the Roman State ; he may have been ignorant of the part played by economic forces in shaping the ultimate catastrophe—a fact of which modern historians are now fully conscious ; nevertheless, the general principles he emphasized have at least this importance, that they formed the point of departure for subsequent investigators, the background of the subject, so to speak, against which we paint our fuller and more adequate pictures.

There is one matter, moreover, in which Gibbon registered a great advance upon Montesquieu and rendered a signal service to scholarship, viz. in the care with which he investigated the part played by Christianity in the great drama. The *Grandeur et Decadence des Romains* has nothing to say on the subject of religion either Christian or pagan. To Gibbon, on the other hand, it was a topic of capital importance. " As I believed, and as I still believe," he noted in the *Autobiography*,[1] " that the propagation of the Gospel, and the

[1] Page 183.

triumph of the Church, are inseparably connected with the decline of the Roman monarchy, I weighed the causes and effects of the revolution, and contrasted the narratives and apologies of the Christian themselves, with the glances of candour or enmity which the Pagans have cast on the rising sects." Are we to assume, then, that Gibbon numbered the Christian religion among the forces making for the destruction of Rome ? Professor Bury is emphatic on the point, not only that he so regarded it, but also that he gave it the first place among the disruptive elements. According to Gibbon, runs his verdict,[1] " The historical development of human societies since the second century after Christ, was a retrogression *for which Christianity was mainly to blame."* The suggestion is plausible, if descriptive of the spirit and intention with which Gibbon wrote ; but those who accept it would find it difficult to adduce any passage from the *Decline and Fall* which, taken in its entirety and with reference to its context, lends any real support for the thesis. The sentence quoted by Professor Bury in conjunction with the remark just cited —" I have described the triumph of barbarism and religion " —when read in its proper context, is seen to be merely the Gibbonian way of saying that he has traced the history of the Gothic conquests and the rise of the Church.[2] Of course, the use of the word " triumph " is peculiar : it implies a sneer, and clearly reflects the deep current of hostility to Christianity, which ran beneath Gibbon's placid and scholarly calm. In common with all the rationalists of the eighteenth century he disliked the Christian religion as a superstitious growth, fostered in a barbarous age, and productive of fanaticism, intolerance, and discord. His entire history is saturated with this temperamental and intellectual antipathy ; it breaks out continually in cold indifference, sarcastic insinuation, or thinly veiled contempt. Milman puts it very moderately [3] when he says that " Christianity alone receives no embellishment from the magic of Gibbon's language, his imagination is dead to its moral dignity ; it is

[1] Introduction to *Decline and Fall*, p. xxxviii.
[2] *Decline and Fall*, vii, p. 308.
[3] Preface to *Decline and Fall*.

kept down by a general tone of disparagement, or neutralized by a painfully elaborate exposition of its darker and degenerate periods." But it will be evident that the disparagement of Christianity is quite a different thing from singling it out as the chief destructive agency in the decline of Rome. What Gibbon actually asserts is that the calamities afflicting or threatening the empire were imputed *by the pagans* to the religion of Christ and of Constantine.[1] That he himself did not share this view is evident from a subsequent comment, in which he points out that, even in its most corrupt state, Christianity taught the barbarian justice, mercy, and fidelity, and by its humane sentiments helped to alleviate the horrors of war, to moderate the violence of conquest, and " *to preserve in the downfall of the empire, a permanent respect for the name and institutions of Rome."* [2] A religion which accomplished this could not be called simply destructive. But the most balanced and mature opinion expressed by Gibbon on the subject of Christianity's influence on the fate of the empire is to be found in the general summary at the close of Chapter XXXVIII. Here he sets down the *pros* and *cons* with remarkable detachment ; and we may assume that it represents his final conclusion on the matter. Observe the caution of the opening sentence : " As the happiness of a future life is the great object of religion, we may hear without surprise or scandal, that the introduction, or *at least the abuse*, of Christianity had *some* influence on the decline and fall of the Roman Empire." [3] Then follows the indictment. Christianity was responsible for the discouragement of the active virtues of society and the inculcation of patience and humility, for the diversion of public money to the upkeep of anti-social institutions like monasticism, for the distraction of Church and State by the " flame of theological discord," and for the deflection of the emperor's attention from camps to synods. But against this negative side of the account he sets the positive. " Party spirit," he proceeds,[4] " however pernicious or absurd, is a *principle of union* as well as of dissension. The bishops from 1800 pulpits, *inculcated the duty*

---

[1] *Decline and Fall*, III, p. 193. [2] *Ibid.*, VI, p. 80.
[3] *Ibid.*, IV, p. 162. [4] *Ibid.*, p. 163.

of passive obedience to a lawful and orthodox sovereign ; their frequent assemblies and perpetual correspondence maintained the communion of distant churches : and the benevolent temper of the gospel was strengthened, though confined, by the spiritual alliance of the catholics. The sacred indolence of the monks was devoutly embraced by a servile and effeminate age ; but *if superstition had not afforded a decent retreat, the same vices would have tempted the unworthy Romans to desert, from baser motives, the standard of the republic. . .* If the decline of the Roman empire was hastened by the conversion of Constantine, his *victorious religion broke the fall and mollified the ferocious temper of the conquerors."*

In the face of these latter admissions and qualifications it would be unfair to conclude that Gibbon believed only in the negative influence of Christianity. He realized that although the spirit of the Christian religion was inimical to the whole structure of ancient society, and therefore proved to be an element of weakness when established as the official *credo,* yet its constructive genius held the world together (much in the same way as feudalism held the early mediaeval world together) during the period of decline, and so saved humanity from the worst evils when the collapse actually occurred. Moreover, if Gibbon's contention is right that Rome's downfall was due simply to the operation of a kind of natural law —" the natural and inevitable effect of immoderate greatness "—neither the barbarian nor the Christian can have had any vital part in the catastrophe. As a matter of fact, the worst charge he flings against the Christians is that they destroyed many architectural masterpieces of antiquity in order to build churches.[1] But even here the acerbity of his judgment is tempered with the reflection that the major part of the destruction took place during the bitter family feuds of the Middle Ages.[2]

It is worth while remarking that, at the close of his observations on the subject of Rome's collapse, when he has sifted all the facts, and brought the whole sequence of events, as it were, *sub specie æternitatis,* Gibbon falls into a singularly mellow and reflective mood, in which he is prepared to forget

[1] *Ibid.,* VII, pp. 309-10.   [2] *Ibid.,* pp. 314-15-16.

and forgive all the crimes committed against the empire.
" We may," he avers,[1] " acquiesce in the pleasing conviction
that every age of the world has increased, and still increases,
the real wealth, the happiness, the knowledge, and perhaps
the virtue of the human race." In other words, when all is
said and done, history does not register retrogression as the
sole characteristic of any epoch, but both retrogression and
progress ; and, on the whole, the progress has been more
noticeable.

HIS STYLE

It is, strictly speaking, beyond the limits of this study to
enter into a discussion of Gibbon's style ; the topic belongs to
the province of literature rather than of history. Nevertheless, the qualities of the *Decline and Fall*, viewed from the
literary standpoint, are so uniquely and integrally a part of
its author's genius and success that a special plea may be put
forward for considering it here. Stylistically—using the
word in its widest signification—it may safely be assumed that
Gibbon drew his inspiration from antiquity and not from
the modern world. His favourite authors were the great
historians of Rome, Livy and Tacitus. The comments he
passes on them are illuminating, partly because of the shrewd
judgments they contain, but mainly because of the light they
throw on his own conception of how history should be written.
Of Livy he speaks with enthusiasm.[2] The majestic yet rapid
flow of his narrative, his energy and beauty, his graphic
touch, his epic dignity seemed to Gibbon the perfect model
of historical composition. At the same time, he fully
recognized that accuracy was not Livy's *forte* : he is, writes
the author of the *Decline and Fall*, a poor witness, careless in
points of geography, unacquainted with the art of war, and
in every respect a typical man of letters " covered with the
dust of his library ."[3] For factual information he much
preferred Polybius—the man of action, familiar with the
military profession, who described that he knew in language
of " unadorned simplicity and plain reason." [4] But his chief

---

[1] *Ibid.*, iv, p. 169.　　　[2] *Miscellaneous Works*, II, pp. 182-3.
[3] *Ibid.*, p. 183.　　　[4] *Ibid.*

affection was centred on Tacitus, the " first of historians who applied the science of philosophy to the study of facts." [1] Unlike Voltaire, who dismissed the *Annals* as a satire, he found in them one of the world's masterpieces in historical literature. Livy had pleased him as a romantic historian who sought to inspire his readers with feelings of pity, awe, or admiration as the drama of Rome unfolded itself ; but Tacitus, with an eye for the human value of events, satisfied his intellectual curiosity by fixing attention on the causal aspect of things. *Je gravis sur les Alpes*, remarks Gibbon, *avec Annibal, mais j'assiste au counseil de Tibère.* [2] In other words, Tacitus' greatness, in his eyes, rests upon the genius he displays in analysing motives and interpreting history.

How far the *Decline and Fall* reflects, in detail, the qualities of the Roman historians is not easy to determine, and must be a matter for conjecture rather than positive assertion. Certain broad resemblances, however, are fairly clear. One cannot, for example, fail to compare Gibbon's narrative splendour, epic grandeur, and dignity of conception with the corresponding characteristics of Livy. With both, the portrayal of a magnificent historical drama in appropriate language, as graphically as the imagination can make it, was the dominant interest and the main guiding principle. On the other hand, a good comparison may be instituted with Tacitus on the score of subtlety in analysis, brilliance of characterization, and general " inwardness " of appeal. Possibly we might say that it was Livy who influenced Gibbon more in the general architecture of his work, and Tacitus who supplied him with a model for its detailed execution.

Much, however, as he owed to his Roman preceptors there is no writer to whom Buffon's immortal saying may be more fitly applied than the author of the *Decline and Fall*—" Style is the man himself." His struggles with the written word are proverbial. From the time of his first serious plunge into literature—the *Essai sur l'Étude de la Littérature*—until he crystallized his mode of literary expression in the history of Rome, his record was, in his own eyes, one of defeat and

---

[1] *Decline and Fall*, I, p. 213.   [2] *Essai sur l'Étude de la Littérature*, lii.

failure. And even when he began his great work it took him some little time to " hit the middle tone between a dull chronicle and a rhetorical declamation." " Three times," he says,[1] " did I compose the first chapter and twice the second and third before I was tolerably satisfied." Thereafter the art of composition sat less heavy upon him ; but there is no reason to believe that Gibbon ever wrote with a flowing pen. To the end he remained a tense writer, to whom the utmost care and deliberation were a second nature. Nothing was committed to paper that failed to stand the double test of accuracy and euphony. His unit was the paragraph, which was first blocked out, rearranged, and tested at all points *mentally*, before the final shredding down into sentences took place.[2] Only when his ear told him that he had achieved æsthetic perfection did he take up the pen and write. The consequence is that the style of the *Decline and Fall* resembles a Ciceronian oration ; it is deliberate, robust, agile with a leisurely ponderous agility, which makes the utmost demand upon the reader, and never leaves him free to relax his mind or indulge in *reveries*. The author is too much with us, perpetually insisting that he, and not we, have the direction of affairs in hand. It is impossible to read him with a slack imagination or a drowsy intellect ; one's faculties must always be on the stretch pursuing his allusions, weighing up his epithets, exploring his antitheses.[3]

There is, of course, much to be said for such a style as a means of describing an exalted and splendid historical panorama. The gravity and dignity, the pomp and circumstance of the utterance are in keeping with the grandeur of the theme ; and few readers who immerse themselves in it would willingly exchange if for another. It is surprising, too, how much variety Gibbon contrives to introduce into his sentences, in spite of their general stiffness and lack of pliancy. He can be picturesque, dramatic, satirical, allusive, ironical, laconic, epigrammatic, sententious—in fact, he is capable of sounding most of the notes that lie within the gamut of

---

[1] *Autobiography*, p. 190. [2] *Ibid.*, p. 201.
[3] Harrison, *Centenary of Gibbon* : " It is impossible to hurry through your Gibbon ; you cannot skip ; you cannot take in a description at a glance ; you cannot leave out the adjectives, or jump to the second half of a clause."

the literary man. The only stops he cannot use are emotion and sentiment ; his appeal is to the brain rather than the heart of his readers.[1] But this was due to defect of temperament, and is compensated by his excellence in other directions. His greatest asset is dry, sardonic humour, which plays round his sentences like summer lightning, or transfixes characters and incidents with deadly effect. A little reflection will show that far from being a mere mannerism, or artificially concocted *façon de parler*, Gibbon's irony is part and parcel of his attitude to the world. When human affairs are viewed from a sufficiently detached standpoint they must always assume the aspect of a comedy or tragi-comedy, an elaborately constructed play in which the poor players strut and fret their hour upon the stage and then are swallowed into silence. It was, moreover, all in Gibbon's favour that he chose a theme, which accentuated, more than most, this tragi-comic aspect of existence. Even if he had not been originally endowed with a certain acerbity of temper and dryness of humour it is probable that the contemplation of more than a thousand years of human history would have induced it. But we know it was customary with him to moralize, as he wrote, on the doings of the puppets his pen set in motion. " A being of the nature of man," he comments, at the close of his summary of Byzantine history,[2] " endowed with the same faculties, but with a longer measure of existence, would cast down a smile of pity and contempt on the crimes and follies of human ambition, so eager, in a narrow space, to grasp at a precarious and short-lived enjoyment. It is thus that the experience of history exalts and enlarges the horizon of our intellectual view. In a composition of some days, in a perusal of some hours, six hundred years have rolled away, and the duration of a life or a reign is contracted to a fleeting moment : the grave is ever beside the throne : the success of the criminal is almost instantly followed by the loss of the prize : and our immortal reason survives and disdains the sixty phantoms of

---

[1] " Gibbon cannot be numbered among the great painters of human nature, for he has no sympathy with the heart and passions of our race."—Bagehot, *op. cit.*

[2] *Decline and Fall*, V, pp. 242-3.

kings who have passed before our eyes and faintly dwell on our remembrance."

There is, a danger of course, in so Olympian an attitude : it tends to make history too subjective. Facts are presented as they appear to be when viewed athwart the prism of the writer's imagination. Individuals are represented by a kind of subtle caricature, or sketched with broad splashes of colour, their virtues and vices exaggerated, their motives belauded or besmirched as the case may be ; and it dawns upon the mind of the reader that what he is engaged upon is not a reflection of reality, but a brilliant literary picture, a shadow show, in which the puppets are controlled by the strings of the operator. So it is with Gibbon. There is caricature in many of his characterizations, a tendency to balance his characters on the needle point for the delectation of his readers, to dismiss them with a brilliant epigram, or to draw out certain features with a view to rendering them ridiculous. But with all his faults he must be ranked as one of the very greatest, if not the greatest, of historical portrait painters. For mordant wit, it would be hard to equal his sketches of Gallienus,[1] John of Cappadocia,[2] Severus,[3] Manuel Comnenus,[4] Justinian II,[5] or Constantine Copronymus[6] ; a few lines boldly drawn and the individual stands out from the canvas as sharply as if some necromancer had summoned his shade from " the vasty deep." But the calm

[1] " In every art that he attempted, his lively genius enabled him to succeed ; and as his genius was destitute of judgment, he attempted every art except the important ones of war and government. He was a master of several curious but useless sciences, a ready orator, an eloquent poet, a skilful gardener, an excellent cook, and a most contemptible prince."—*Decline and Fall*, I, pp. 273-4.

[2] " His aspiring fortune was raised on the death of thousands, the poverty of millions, the ruin of cities, and the desolation of provinces."—*Ibid.*, II, pp. 240-1.

[3] " He promised only to betray, he flattered only to deceive, and however he might occasionally bind himself by oaths and treaties, his conscience, obsequious to his interest, always released him from the inconvenient obligation."—*Ibid.*, I, p. 116.

[4] *Ibid.*, V, p. 231.

[5] " His favourite ministers were two beings the least susceptible of human sympathy, an eunuch and a monk ; to the one he abandoned the palace, to the other the finances ; the former corrected the emperor's mother with a scourge, the latter suspended the insolent tributaries with their heads downwards over a smoky fire."—*Ibid.*, V, p. 179.

[6] " His reign was a long butchery of whatever was noble, or holy, or innocent, in his empire."—*Ibid.*, V, p. 186.

steady light he diffuses over the portraits of Ambrose,[1] Athanasius,[2] Julian,[3] Justinian I,[4] Belisarius,[5] Aurelius,[6] Gregory I,[7] Stilicho,[8] Theodosius,[9] Leo IV,[10] or Basil I,[11] is no less wonderful. Genius, statesmanship, humanity, courage, never failed to awaken Gibbon's interest, nor did vice, tortuousness, or brutality ever escape his pillory. Like Voltaire, he sits as judge over human character, praising, excusing, censuring, and condemning with a remarkable approach to even-handed justice.

Equally important with his skill in characterization must be reckoned Gibbon's descriptive brilliance. His peculiar excellence in this department is that he never indulges in poetic licence : his most brilliant flights, when reduced to their elements, are simply collections of facts thrown together with the minimum of cement. Chapter and verse could be quoted for every stroke of the pen. It is in this smelting together of hundreds of scattered details that his genius as a literary artist largely consists. " He was," says Frederic Harrison,[12] " the consummate literary artist, who transmutes mountains of exact research into a complex mass glowing with life in all its parts, and glorious to contemplate as a whole." One of his most effective descriptions in his account of the Crusaders' approach to Constantinople in 1204 ; it runs as follows : [13]

While the wind was favourable, the sky serene, and the water smooth, every eye was fixed with wonder and delight on the scene of military pomp which overspread the sea. The shields of the knights and squires, at once an ornament and a defence, were arranged on either side of the ships : and the banners of the nations and families were displayed from the stern ; our modern artillery was supplied by three hundred engines for casting stones and darts : the fatigues of the way were cheered with the sound of music ; and the spirits of the adventurers were raised by the mutual assurance that forty thousand christian heroes were equal to the conquest of the earth. . . . As they passed along, they

[1] *Ibid.*, III, pp. 155-161.   [2] *Ibid.*, II, pp. 361-4.   [3] *Ibid.*, II, p. 430.
[4] *Ibid.*, IV, p. 430-2.   [5] *Ibid.*, p. 429.   [6] *Ibid.*, I, pp. 77-8.
[7] *Ibid.*, V, pp. 33-5.   [8] *Ibid.*, III, pp. 224-6.   [9] *Ibid.*, III, pp. 121-2.
[10] *Ibid.*, VI, p. 41.   [11] *Ibid.*, V, pp. 204-6.
[12] *Centenary of Gibbon.*   [13] *Decline and Fall*, VI, pp. 390-L

gazed with admiration on the capital of the East, or, as it should
seem, of the earth, rising from her seven hills, and towering over
the continents of Europe and Asia. The swelling domes and
lofty spires of five hundred palaces and churches were gilded by
the sun and reflected in the waters ; the walls were crowded with
soldiers and spectators, whose numbers they beheld, of whose
temper they were ignorant ; and each heart was chilled by the
reflection that, since the beginning of the world, such an enterprise
had never been undertaken by such a handful of warriors. But
the momentary apprehension was dispelled by hope and valour ;
and every man, says the marshal of Champagne, glanced his eye
on the sword or lance which he must speedily use in the glorious
conflict.

More subtle, but no less effective from the artistic point of
view, is his celebrated description of monastic life in Egypt.[1]
The passage is noteworthy, not only for the information it
imparts, but also for the atmosphere with which it is suffused.
Without interrupting the even flow of his narrative to pass
any disparaging comment, Gibbon contrives to insinuate into
it a deprecatory air, composed partly of pity, partly of contempt ; and the result is that the reader is left both with a
record of fact and with a judgment.   In other words, what we
have is a clever psychological study of the effects of monastic
seclusion on the human mind—its miseries, its illusions, and
profound boredom.   The passage runs as follows :

According to their faith and zeal, they (i.e. the monks) might
employ the day, which they passed in their cells, either in vocal
or mental prayer ; they assembled in the evening, and they were
awakened in the night, for the public worship of the monastery.
The precise moment was determined by the stars, which are
seldom clouded in the serene sky of Egypt ; and a rustic horn
or trumpet, the signal of devotion, twice interrupted the vast
silence of the desert. Even sleep, *the last refuge of the unhappy*,
was rigorously measured ; the vacant hours of the monk heavily
rolled along, without business or pleasure ; and before the close
of each day, he had repeatedly accused the tedious progress of
the Sun. *In this comfortless state*, superstition still pursued and
tormented her wretched votaries. The repose which they had

[1] *Ibid.*, IV, pp. 71-2.

sought in the cloister was disturbed by tardy repentance, profane doubts, and guilty desires ; and while they considered each natural impulse as an unpardonable sin, they perpetually trembled on the edge of a flaming and bottomless abyss. From the painful struggles of disease and despair *these unhappy victims* were sometimes relieved by madness or death ; and, in the sixth century, a hospital was founded at Jerusalem for a small portion of the austere penitents, who were deprived of their senses. Their visions, before they attained this extreme and acknowledged term of frenzy, have afforded ample materials of supernatural history. It was their firm persuasion that the air which they breathed was peopled with invisible enemies ; with innumerable dæmons, who watched every occasion, and assumed every form, to terrify, and above all to tempt, their unguarded virtue. The imagination, and even the senses, were deceived by the illusions of distempered fanaticism ; and the hermit, whose midnight prayer was oppressed by involuntary slumber, might easily confound the phantoms of horror or delight which had occupied his sleeping and his waking dreams"[1]

Much of Gibbon's attractiveness as a historical writer is due to adventitious aids and devices, which must seem somewhat tawdry to the purist. Thus, for example, he bodies out sentences with picturesque assemblages of sonorous names, and goes out of his way to charm the reader with the impressiveness of his word music,[2] or to stimulate his imagination by the associations and allusions which the words call up.[3]

[1] By common consent Chaps. L (Arabia and Mahomet) and LVI (The Normans in S. Italy) are recognized as the most brilliant. But the following passages might also be noted as outstanding : I, pp. 345 (Amphitheatre of Titus) and 310 (Triumph of Aurelius) ; II, pp. 361 (Julian's march to Constantinople), 389-90 (Diocletian's palace at Salona), 466 (the temple of Daphne), 490 (Julian's campaign in Persia) ; III, p. 440 (Banquet of Attila) ; IV, pp. 231 (Silk trade of East), 244-8 (St. Sophia) ; VI, pp. 152 (Russian trade with Byzantium), 140-1 (the Hungarians) ; VII, Chap. LXVIII (the Capture of Constantinople by Mahomet II).

[2] E.g. I, p. 24.

[3] E.g. I, p. 260 : "The banks of the Borysthenes are only sixty miles distant from the narrow entrance of the peninsula of Crim Tartary, known to the ancients under the name of Chersonesus Taurica. On that inhospitable shore, Euripides, embellishing with exquisite art the tales of antiquity, has placed the scene of one of his most affecting tragedies. The bloody sacrifices of Diana, the arrival of Orestes and Pylades, and the triumph of virtue and religion over savage fierceness serve to represent an historical truth, that the Tauri, the original inhabitants of the peninsula, were in some degree reclaimed from their brutal manners by a gradual intercourse with the Grecian colonies which settled along the maritime coast." Cf. also II, pp. 142-3 : "The winding channel through which the waters of the Euxine flow with a rapid and incessant course towards the Mediterranean received the appellation

Similarly, he will not give geographical features their modern names if the classical are more euphonious. The Dneiper becomes the " Borysthenes "; the Theiss, the " Tibiscus "; Scotland, " Caledonia "; the Arctic, the " Hyperborean Ocean." Epic epithets are scattered with a lavish hand through his pages—the " tall Burgundians," the " Heruli of the distant ocean," the " equitable Nerva," the " sublime Longinus," the " generous Atticus," the " eloquent Lactantius," the " learned Aurelius." The Danube, again, is always " frozen," Caledonia must have its " blue mists." Egypt is not complete without its " sultry plains," Libanus must be " snowy," Arabia *Felix* has its " spicy groves," and all mountains are " craggy." But in spite of the artificiality which may be alleged against these tricks of style, there is no doubt that they help materially—and this must be their justification—to carry the reader forward over the enormous tract of time and space spanned by the *Decline and Fall.* Narrative is the most difficult of all the elements in historical composition; and if Gibbon accomplished the task better than any other historian it is but a poor and bankrupt criticism that pries into his method too closely.

Infinitely more important are the real flaws in the Gibbonian style which cannot be glossed over or explained away; they strike the reader as soon as he has proceeded a short way into the History. The first and most obvious of these is the inappropriateness of Gibbon's diction when he descends from the august to the simple. Historical truth is of many kinds or degrees: it may be grand or humble, gorgeous or plain, complex or simple, romantic or sordid, solemn or humorous, etc. Men cannot be for ever heroic, or movements always inspiring; there are periods when both become dull, drab,

---

ot Bosphorus, a name not less celebrated in the history than in the fables of antiquity. A crowd of temples and of votive altars profusely scattered along its steep and woody banks, attested the unskilfulness of the Grecian navigators, who after the example of the Argonauts, explored the dangers of the inhospitable Euxine. On these banks tradition long preserved the memory of the palace of Phineus, infested by the obscene harpies; and of the sylvan reign of Amycus, who defied the son of Leda to the combat of the Cestus." etc. And VI, p. 486 : " The olive tree, the gift of Minerva, flourishes in Attica ; nor has the honey of Mount Hymettus lost any part of its exquisite flavour ; but the languid trade is monopolized by strangers, and the agriculture of a barren land is abandoned to the vagrant Wallachians."

or even mean. There are occasions, moreover, when purely factual explanations are indispensable, and nothing else will do. Clearly it would be incongruous to describe the composition of gunpowder or the manufacture of silk, or a piece of artillery, in the same way in which one describes a battle, a *levée*, or a triumphal procession. The historian must be prepared to discriminate between the incidents and characters that fall under his notice, and to modify his style accordingly. But it is here that Gibbon displays his weakness most conspicuously. As one critic remarks, he cannot say Asia *minor*.[1] His stiffly brocaded style cannot unbend sufficiently to grapple with simple things. When we read, for example, that silk " composes the golden tomb from which a worm emerges in the form of a butterfly"[2] or that the Roman artillery cast stones and darts with irresistible violence " in an oblique or horizontal manner,"[3] we feel that whatever the merits of the grand style may be when applied to great events, it is not particularly informative about plain matters of fact. Or, again, when we read that " a thousand swords were plunged *at once* into the bosom of the unfortunate Probus,"[4] or that " a string of camels laden with corn and provisions, covered *almost without an interval* the long road from Memphis to Medina,"[5] we realize that it is better fitted to procure effects than to state the unadorned truth. Sometimes pure melodrama is the result of using it, as in the following account of the Vikings:[6] " The vast, and, it is said, the populous regions of Denmark, Sweden, and Norway, were crowded with independent chieftains, who *sighed in the laziness of peace and smiled in the agonies of death.* . . . Impatient of a bleak climate and narrow limits, they *started from the banquet, grasped their arms, sounded their horn, ascended their vessels,* and explored every coast that promised either spoil or settlement."

In addition to this flaw, which is really the defect of a virtue, Gibbon's style may be criticized as introducing into historical writing the first beginnings of a jargon. There are certain expressions which he falls back upon periodically as

---

[1] Bagehot : *Literary Studies*, I, p. 227. [2] *Decline and Fall*, IV, p. 228.
[2] *Ibid.*, I, p. 15. [4] *Ibid.*, p. 337.
[3] *Ibid.*, V, p. 456. [6] *Ibid.*, VI, p. 148.

a kind of standard diction, and their reiteration becomes tiresome and at times even meaningless. How frequently, for instance, occur the words "specious," "complacent," "insensible," or variations of the phrase "assume the purple"? How often does he "proceed to" interrogate, "affect to" deplore, "deign to" consult? How often do his characters "sigh," "blush," or "smile with contempt"? It may be, of course, that every scientific study must evolve a formality of expression; and history, being a branch of scientific inquiry, must fall in with the general trend. Nevertheless, the formalizing of expression, or, as we prefer to call it, jargon, if carried to any extent, means the withdrawal of history from the realm of literature, and Gibbon, at any rate, would have deprecated any such result. Probably all who stand for humanism in history would take a similar view.

INDEX

Acton, Lord, 8, 10
Addison, 20
Alison, Sir A., 130
Amari, 20
America, History of, 121, 133, 136, 137, 138. See also under *Robertson*
Autobiography (of Gibbon), 147–55, 159; (of Hume), 83

Bagehot, 143, 144, 145, 176 n., 182 n.
Balbo, 11
Balfour, Lord, 168, 169
Barker, Dr. E., 12
Baudrillart, 45 n., 46
Bengesco, G., 64, 71
Bernheim, 3 n, 8 n., 56 n.
Bodin, 45
Bolingbroke, 31
Bonar, 16 n.
Bossuet, 26, 61, 72, 73, 151
Boufflers, Comtesse de, 91
Brougham, Lord, 70, 123, 125, 140 n.
Brunetière, 23
Buckle, 1, 59
Buffon, 18
Burton, J. H., 17 n., 30, 81, 93
Bury, Prof., 4, 9, 146, 163, 164, 170

Catherine, Empress of Russia, 15
Causeries du Lundi, 2, 144
Charles V., 15, 130. See also under *Robertson*.
Charles XII, 14; *Preface*, 32–3
Châtelet, Marquise du, 33, 34
Chesterfield, Lord, 117
Columbus, Life of, 125
Condorcet, 29
Croce, 13, 27 n.

Decline and Fall, 15, 144, 145, 163–73. See also under *Gibbon*
Deism, 25
Descartes, 18
Discours sur Méthode, 23 n.

Enlightenment, 22–5; in England, 25, 26; in France, 26–8
Esprit des Lois, 45
Essai sur l'Étude de la Littérature, 152, 157, 158 n.
Essai sur les Mœurs, 33, 38, 45. See also under *Voltaire*
Ethical judgments in history, 3, 6, 7

Faguet, 38 n., 44, 57
Fontenelle, 23, 24
Freeman, 10
Fueter, 71, 78

Garrick, 15
Geffroy, 63, 64
German historians in the nineteenth century, 10, 11
Gibbon: his popularity, 15; ignorance of palæography, 16; anxiety for stylistic perfection, 17; praise of Robertson, 117; diligence and accuracy, 145; approach to the history of Rome, 146–56; his positive mind, 147; early reading, 148, 149; leisurely method, 149; turning-points in his career, 150–55; at Oxford, 150, 151; at Lausanne, 151, 153, 154; study of Latin literature, 152; second visit to Lausanne, 153; study of Italian geography, 153 154; proposes to write a book on the geography of Italy, 154;